D1153671

The Spiritual Art
of Raising Children
with Disabilities

KATHLEEN   DEYER   BOLDUC

Foreword by Ginny Thornburgh

Afterword by William Gaventa

Judson Press has made every effort to trace the ownership of all quotes. In the event of a question arising from the use of a quote, we regret any error made and will be pleased to make the necessary correction in future printings and editions of this book.

Scripture quotations are from the following translations:
AMP indicates the Amplified® Bible, copyright © 1954, 1958, 1962, 1964, 1965, 1987 by The Lockman Foundation. Used by permission.
ESV indicates The Holy Bible, English Standard Version® (ESV®), copyright © 2001 by Crossway, a publishing ministry of Good News Publishers. Used by permission. All rights reserved.
MSG indicates THE MESSAGE. Copyright © by Eugene H. Peterson 1993, 1994, 1995, 1996, 2000, 2001, 2002. Used by permission of NavPress Publishing Group.
NIV indicates HOLY BIBLE, NEW INTERNATIONAL VERSION®. NIV®. Copyright © 1973, 1978, 1984, 2011 by Biblica, Inc.™ Used by permission. All rights reserved worldwide.
NLT indicates Holy Bible, New Living Translation, copyright © 1996. Used by permission of Tyndale House Publishers, Inc., Wheaton, IL 60189. All rights reserved.
NRSV indicates the New Revised Standard Version Bible, copyright © 1989 by the Division of Christian Education of the National Council of the Churches of Christ in the United States of America. Used by permission. All rights reserved.
RSV indicates the Revised Standard Version Bible, copyright © 1952, Division of Christian Education of the National Council of the Churches of Christ in the United States of America. Used by permission. All rights reserved.
VOICE indicates The Voice Bible. Copyright © 2012 Thomas Nelson, Inc. The Voice translation™ © 2012 Ecclesia Bible Society. Used by permission. All rights reserved.
Scripture quotations from The Living Bible, © 1971. Used by permission of Tyndale House Publishers, Inc., Wheaton, Illinois 60189. All rights reserved.

Cover and interior design by Wendy Ronga and Hampton Design.
Cover mosaic and interior images by Kristen Gebhardt.

Library of Congress Cataloging-in-Publication data
Cataloging-in-Publication Data available upon request. Contact cip@judsonpress.com.

Printed in the U.S.A.
First Edition, 2014.

Foreword

Some books make you laugh. Others make you cry. Occasionally, a book will cause something deep inside your spirit to vibrate with a sense of recognition: *This author knows; she knows what it is like to stumble along in my shoes; she knows and understands.* Rarely does one book evoke all three.

The Spiritual Art of Raising Children with Disabilities is one of those rare treasures—a book that offers the surprise of unexpected laughter, the unlooked-for permission to weep, and the tender empathy of a stranger who knows. Kathleen Deyer Bolduc has walked a lifetime in shoes worn through by parents of children with disabilities. She knows the joys and sorrows that caring for such special children brings. She knows the exhilaration of minute victories and the exhaustion of mammoth challenges. She knows the overwhelming love and the deep longings; she comprehends the ferocious faith required to persevere through one frustration after another.

In this spiritually uplifting book, Kathy acknowledges the experience of brokenness that comes to all human beings—and especially to those entrusted with the task of raising children with disabilities. She spreads out the fragments of once-cherished hopes, dreams, and expectations. She shares the stories of her own experience, raising a son with multiple special needs while nurturing two other children, a marriage, and her own spirit. And she engages the stories told by others, inviting them to relate not only their real-life challenges but also the real-world strategies and life-giving insights that have sustained them as parents, as spouses, as human beings, and as children of God.

The chapters are short—crafted with the chaos of life in mind. They are accented with poems and epigraphs that sparkle with power and profound wisdom. They are framed by personal anecdotes and scriptural encourage-

Foreword

ment. They are held together with compassion and creativity, and crowned with concrete, contemplative practices to reconnect our spirit to the Holy Spirit who is the Source of our strength and hope and peace and joy.

Parents, grandparents, and other caregivers will revel in the spiritual refreshment and renewal offered in these pages. Family members and friends, teachers and clergy, who care for and work with children with disabilities, will all find here a window into the hearts and spirits of their parents. Spiritual directors and coaches will welcome this resource as a practical tool for ministry to and with parents who desperately seek resurrection and wholeness in their faith journey.

Kathy writes as a certified spiritual director herself; she writes as a mother; she writes as a woman of faith. And in all of that, Kathy is also an artist. Even as she offers the metaphor of the mosaic as an image of the life we craft, raising children with disabilities, Kathy has herself created a literary mosaic—her stories, the children's stories, the parents' stories, all pieced together as part of God's story. And the result is nothing short of a masterpiece!

—Ginny Thornburgh
Director, AAPD Interfaith Initiative
American Association of People with Disabilities

Acknowledgments

I AM THANKFUL FOR THE PARTNERSHIP, SUPPORT, AND FRIENDSHIP OF THE FOLLOWING PEOPLE:

Jana Riess, for planting the seed that grew into this book.

My friends at Judson Press, for believing in the importance of the topic, and my editor, Cassandra Williams, for her critical eye yet kind and gentle way with my words.

Alysia, Cindi, Dave, Rob, Thom, Bonnie, Anne, Barbara, Margo, Glenn, Kim, Ginny, Barb, and Gail, for taking the time to talk with me and for the transparency with which you shared your stories. May your words go out as blessing.

Kristen Gebhardt, for an awesome mosaic for the cover of this book.

My teacher of spiritual direction, Dave Nixon, and the entire cohort with whom I studied, for your gifts of listening, laughter, and persistence in asking good questions.

Patti Gordon, my spiritual director, for walking alongside me.

Jackie Matisse and Cheryl Schaeffner, for the weekly gift of time together in *lectio* and prayer.

Katie Reid, for so many shared meals during the writing of this book, and for igniting a passion for sharing *lectio divina* with the world.

Acknowledgments

Mike Woods, for inviting me to be a part of the blogging community at specialneedsparenting.org, and to all of my fellow parent bloggers there. You are awesome!
Patty Kyrlach, Kay Clark, Robyn Whitlock, and Michele Huey, for critiquing this manuscript from start to finish, and The Writing Academy, for 30-plus years of support.

My mother, Virginia Deyer, for her enthusiastic and loving support.

My sons, Matt and Justin Bolduc, and daughters-of-heart, Elizabeth Bolduc and Sarah Adams, for blessing my life with your presence.

Wally Bolduc, my husband, for reminding me that laughter and play are essential elements of the kingdom.

And my son, Joel Bolduc, for bringing me, day by day, before the throne of grace. Without you there would be no book.

To God be the glory!

For this reason I bow my knees before the Father, from whom every family in heaven and on earth takes its name. I pray that, according to the riches of his glory, he may grant that you may be strengthened in your inner being with power through his Spirit, and that Christ may dwell in your hearts through faith, as you are being rooted and grounded in love. I pray that you may have the power to comprehend, with all the saints, what is the breadth and length and height and depth, and to know the love of Christ that surpasses knowledge, so that you may be filled with all the fullness of God. Now to him who by the power at work within us is able to accomplish abundantly far more than all we can ask or imagine, to him be glory in the church and in Christ Jesus to all generations, forever and ever. Amen.

—Ephesians 3:14-21, NRSV

Introduction

Each of us becomes the artist as we allow ourselves to be open to the reality of the Other and give expression to that encounter either in words or paint or stone or in the fabric of our lives. Each of us who has come to know and relate to the Other and expresses this in any way is an artist in spite of himself/herself.... Genuine religion and art are two names for the same incredible meeting with reality and give expression to that experience in some manner.
—Morton T. Kelsey, *The Other Side of Silence:*
A Guide to Christian Meditation[1]

Twenty-five years ago, when my son Joel was a toddler, I woke up one day with the knowledge, deep in my gut, that I did not have what it takes to parent a child with a disability. We didn't have a diagnosis of autism yet. What we did know was that our youngest son wasn't developing according to the timetable followed by his two older brothers. He didn't roll over, sit up, walk, or talk on time. His social skills did not develop appropriately. And his behavior! He had constant meltdowns and tantrums, he pulled hair, and he had a miniscule attention span with a constant need for attention and redirection.

I opened my eyes that morning knowing there was no way, in my humanness, that I could do this right. I simply didn't have the vast reserves of energy, creativity, wisdom, and insight needed to be the mother Joel's needs required.

What I did have was love for my son, love for my family, and love for God.

That day, after Joel's preschool bus wheezed away from the house, I sat down to meditate, a practice I'd taken up after my father had died six years earlier. I began repeating my centering phrase, "Maranatha; come, Lord Jesus," hoping it would help me move through bone-crushing anxiety to a place of peace. I found myself, instead, having a heated one-way conversation with God.

Are you there, God? Are you listening? I can't do this on my own! I'm handing him over, Lord. He's yours. And you're going to have to show me how to mother this child, because the mothering skills I've learned over the past ten years with Joel's brothers just aren't doing the trick. I'm helpless here, Lord. Are you there? Are you listening?

Parenting a child with a disability or chronic illness is hard work. It will most likely be the hardest work we will encounter in our lives. Keeping up with the research alone is a job that could swallow a person alive. Add to that negotiating daily life—trips to the grocery store (disruption of routine), doing the laundry (chaos), serving family meals (beware the picky eater), getting out the door to go to work (Are you kidding?), and finding the best schools for our children's needs (Help!).

Yet overriding all of the above is our deep and abiding love for our children. Fragile hearts are a condition of our humanity. Our hearts break as we observe our children's struggles and anxieties; watch a nurse hook them up yet again to an IV; see them left out of a neighborhood game; or witness their daily meltdowns, aggressive behaviors, or inability to voice their thoughts and feelings.

And so we work. We work until we're numb, finding the right doctors, the right therapies, the right schools, the right medications and supplements, the right diet, the right parenting techniques. Our to-do lists grow exponentially. We expect the lists to shorten as our children get older, but instead, we find them growing.

And we become very, very tired.

Where do we go for solace? For rest and refreshment? For an infilling of joy? We know where to find those things for our kids, but where do we find them for ourselves?

Henri Nouwen is one of the great spiritual teachers of my life. I never met him in person, but I knew him intimately through his books on the spiritual life and his work with adults with disabilities. In his book *Spiritual Direction: Wisdom for the Long Walk of Faith*, Nouwen defines spiritual direction as a relationship between someone who is seeking after God and one who has already walked this path and is willing to listen to, pray with, and respond with wisdom to the questions the seeker is living with.

Introduction

I have been seeking God in the midst of my son's disability for more than twenty-eight years. Meditating on and writing about this journey has grown into my life's work. This walk with Joel's disability has led me to my own spiritual director and to becoming a spiritual director myself. It is my greatest desire, in the pages of this book, to walk alongside you as you seek answers to the questions that are rising up in your heart, and to help you pay attention to God's presence in your life. I will give you some questions to ponder and some reflections to consider, so that the words on the page will become three-dimensional, turning into lived experience.

The pages of this book are also filled with stories from other parents who have walked similar paths with a child's disability or chronic illness, and who have encountered God along the way.

Best of all, you'll find a treasure chest full of ancient traditions—the spiritual disciplines—for us to explore together. These are traditions that have been a part of the Judeo-Christian experience for thousands of years; traditions that draw us ever closer to God; traditions that heighten compassion for our fellow travelers, fill us to overflowing with the joy of the Holy Spirit, and, amazingly, lower stress at the same time. Could you use a little less stress in your life? I thought so!

Close your eyes and visualize an empty cup. Allow yourself to feel its emptiness. Then, in your mind's eye, see that cup being filled by a pitcher of water. A bottomless pitcher of water. See the water slowly fill the cup until it runs over the rim. Feel the refreshment of an empty cup being filled. *That's* the kind of joy the spiritual disciplines can bring to our fatigued and thirsty minds, bodies, and souls.

As I pondered the theme of this book, an image of a mosaic kept coming to my mind. I began thinking of the way mosaics are fashioned from broken shards of pottery and pieces of splintered glass. There is a certain kind of mosaic, called "memoryware," that is made of "found" objects—buttons, pottery, toy figurines—objects with connections to everyday life. I've been thinking of how the artist fits these pieces together, carefully arranging and rearranging them so that the broken edges piece together like a puzzle, forming a beautiful and elaborate pattern. Mosaics generally are colorful and are often crafted of materials that reflect the light or glow as light passes through. Up close, a mosaic may look like a jumbled series of broken pieces. But when you stand back and view it from a distance, you gain the perspective needed to see the unified whole. Created by hand, mosaics are a way of viewing the world—brokenness in wholeness, wholeness in brokenness.

Merilee Tutcik, member of the Society of American Mosaic Artists, writes, "Mosaics are a metaphor for life. It's all about putting the pieces together."[2] What a wonderful metaphor for our lives as parents of children with disabilities. Think about it. Think about the way our lives are shattered with that first diagnosis. How we wake up the next day realizing that our lives will never be the same again. How we work and work at gathering up the pieces, attempting to rearrange them into the familiar pattern we knew before. How, at the same time, we keep striving to create something new.

If we allow it, God, the master artist, *will* help us bring those broken pieces together. God will, in infinite love and compassion, work alongside us, helping us to rearrange the pieces into an exquisite work that surpasses the beauty of what our lives were before.

Terry Tempest Williams, author of *Finding Beauty in a Broken World*, has been quoted as saying, "Beauty is not an option, but a strategy for survival."[3] And so the overarching metaphor of this book is the mosaic. How do we find beauty in our lives as parents of children with disabilities? How do we, with God's presence in our daily lives, rearrange the fragmented and chaotic pieces of our family into a new and beautiful work of art?

This book is divided into five sections. In section one, "Gathering up the Broken Pieces," we will consider the need to admit our powerlessness to "fix" our child's disability, the importance of learning to *live* the difficult questions and embrace our grief, and how to move on, by the grace of God, by letting go of guilt, blame, and shame.

Section two, "Embracing Our Brokenness," acknowledges the upside-down nature of God's kingdom. It wrestles with the truth that God works through our weaknesses and explores the paradigm of becoming a wounded healer.

Introduction

We will consider the question "How do we rearrange the pieces of our lives to create a brand-new piece of art?" in section three, "Rearranging the Pieces to Make a New Creation." We will examine the spiritual litany found in everyday routines, embrace ways to cultivate gratitude and mindfulness, recall the importance of taking care of ourselves and our marriages, and discover the power released as we redefine success.

Just as when we view a mosaic from a distance a greater clarity and beauty emerges, so, too, with our lives. So in section four, "The Bigger Picture: The Mosaic as Community Art," we will step back and look at life with disability from a community perspective, considering ways in which we can strengthen our walk within the church universal as well as within our neighborhoods and social networks.

Just as the mosaic artist needs tools to create a beautiful piece of art, we need tools to help us negotiate new ways of being as parents or caregivers of children with disabilities. Therefore, in section five, "Tools of the Mosaic Artist: An Introduction to the Spiritual Disciplines," we will survey a selection of the classical spiritual disciplines.

The mosaic metaphor continues throughout each section. Because I realize you, as the mom, dad, grandparent, or caregiver of a child with a disability, do not have a lot of spare time, the chapters within each section are short, each containing:

- a quote or poem
- a brief teaching
- a personal story from the parent of a child with a disability
- a reflection exercise

I like to think we are "found" people, sought after by God, the master artist, to make a wonderfully elaborate pattern of beauty—God's very own piece of "memoryware." Through the art of spiritual direction, by seeking God and living the questions, our lives, once chipped or cracked or broken, are transformed into unique and stunning works of art.

Gathering up the Broken Pieces

Transforming Power,
You are such an expert at recycling,
    making the broken whole,
    redeeming the wayward,
    renewing the worn out.
All of humanity is your personal reclamation project—
recyclable material for new creations in Christ Jesus.
Give us new views and new vision
to discover new purposes for new times.
                    —Cathy Cummings Chisholm,
                       Landscapes of the Heart[4]

1

Admitting Our Powerlessness

Man is born broken. He lives by mending. The grace of God is glue.
—Anne Lamott, *Traveling Mercies: Some Thoughts on Faith*[5]

Have you ever sat on the beach, on that part of the sand where the waves have just receded, where the sand is damp and tightly packed? You take a plastic shovel, or perhaps your hand, and begin to dig. You dig and dig until water begins to burble up from within the sand, finally filling the hole you've so carefully carved out. The poet Kahlil Gibran writes of sorrow carving deep into our beings, leaving more room for joy.[6]

I know what it is to grieve. Parents of children with disabilities grieve the death of a dream—the dreamed-of child for whom they waited so long. My third son, Joel, has autism and moderate intellectual disabilities, along with an anxiety disorder and severe kyphosis of the spine. Everything I valued in my life before Joel's birth had to be rethought and revalued—intelligence, efficiency, logic, self-control. The old rules no longer applied, and my spirit, which craves peace, order, comfort, and security, withered as I struggled to make sense of the seemingly senseless—a beautiful boy with a damaged brain.

I was stuck in denial for a very long time, and when I finally broke free, I raced headlong into anger, self-blame, and depression. Through this grieving process, which lasted several years, I never stopped calling out to God. Even on my darkest days, when my mind was too numb to form a prayer, I repeated four words over and over: "Hear my prayer, Lord. Hear my prayer." The grief itself became my prayer.

In the midst of my brokenness, Jesus was born in my spirit.

The pain I experienced as I grieved Joel's disability broke open the Scriptures for me. I came to understand that Jesus turns the cultural belief—that brokenness is to be avoided at all costs—upside down. Christ challenged me to face and embrace my brokenness, as well as Joel's brokenness, so that God's power might be released within both of us. I came to a gut-level understanding of the Lord's words to Paul in 2 Corinthians 12:9 (NIV): "My grace is sufficient for you, for my power is made perfect in weakness."

Those years of grieving—those years of calling out again and again to God—those years of lament—carved a space in my parched spirit for God's living waters. The details of life with Joel did not change. His neurological impairments still caused behaviors that remained very difficult to deal with—hair pulling, tantrums, an inability to be in large groups of people or to tolerate certain noises. His cognitive disability continued to make learning the easiest of tasks difficult. But life-giving waters began to flow as I caught fleeting glimpses of reasons to rejoice in the midst of it all—Joel's infectious grin, his silly jokes, his compassion for people who were hurting, his spontaneity and unconditional love.

I had long struggled to fit prayer and meditation into my busy daily routine. Suddenly it was no longer a struggle. I simply *made* the time because the waters that welled up in the silence filled all my empty places to overflowing. I couldn't do without it! The dry soil of my life became hydrated and fertile. In *Plan B: Further Quotes on Faith*, Anne Lamott quotes the poet Wendell Berry: "It gets darker and darker, and then Jesus is born."[7]

ELSEWHERE in *Plan B*, Lamott recounts an old Hassidic story of a rabbi who taught his congregation to put Scripture on their hearts by studying the Torah diligently. One day someone in the congregation asked, "Why put Scripture *on* our hearts instead of *in* them?" The rabbi answered, "Only God can put Scripture inside. But reading sacred text can put it on your hearts, and then when your hearts break, the holy words will fall inside."[8] These prove to be prophetic words for me.

I write them in my journal as we barrel down I-65 in the Florida panhandle at 70 mph—my husband, Wally, driving, me in the passenger seat, Joel in the backseat—headed to a beach vacation. Little do I know that as I copy these words from Lamott's book, Joel is headed toward one of the worst manic episodes of his life. And believe me, he has had many. Twenty-four-hour bouts of absolutely no sleep. Extreme agitation. Aggression. A need to be on the move every minute around the clock, even in the middle of the night. This would not prove to be a fun vacation!

Nothing breaks a person's heart like watching a family member disintegrate into mania. But then again, nothing breaks a person's heart like holding a stillborn baby. Like getting a call in the middle of the night with the news that a father, mother, sister, brother, or friend has died. Like struggling to overcome an addiction. Like losing a job and being unable to support your family. Like being diagnosed with a chronic or terminal illness.

No one makes it through this life without experiencing a broken heart. Fragile hearts are a condition of our humanity. And yet Scripture tells us that God's power moves in and through our brokenness:

> When the righteous cry for help, the LORD hears,
> and rescues them from all their troubles.
> The LORD is near to the brokenhearted,
> and saves the crushed in spirit. (Psalm 34:17-18, NRSV)

> You have kept count of my tossings;
> put my tears in your bottle.
> Are they not in your record? (Psalm 56:8, NRSV)

> My flesh and my heart may fail,
> but God is the strength of my heart and my portion forever. (Psalm 73:26, NRSV)

He heals the brokenhearted,
and binds up their wounds. (Psalm 147:3, NRSV)

Fear not, for I am with you;
be not dismayed, for I am your God;
I will strengthen you, I will help you,
I will uphold you with my righteous right hand. (Isaiah 41:10, ESV)

"My grace is sufficient for you, for my power is made perfect in weakness." Therefore I will boast all the more gladly about my weaknesses, so that Christ's power may rest on me. (2 Corinthians 12:9, NIV)

"Peace I leave with you; my peace I give to you. I do not give to you as the world gives. Do not let your hearts be troubled, and do not let them be afraid." (John 14:27, NRSV)

The question is, will we patch up our hearts with great globs of concrete, walling them in and protecting them from further damage? Or will we embrace our broken hearts, hold them tenderly in our hands, and allow the love of Jesus to flow through our tears? Will we let words of Scripture fall into our hearts, releasing the power of the Holy Spirit?

Reflection Exercise

Cut a piece of paper into the shape of a heart. Remember doing this in grade school for Valentine's Day? You fold the paper in half, cut half of a heart, then open the paper to find a whole, beautiful heart in your hands. Remember what a surprise and mystery that was as a child? Write a word or two or draw a symbol to represent a place in your life that feels broken today. Now tear the heart into three, four, or five pieces. Find a quiet place to sit, and hold the pieces of the heart in your hands. Close your eyes and allow yourself to experience the pain of that broken place. When the feelings come, give them to God, and ask God to show you something new. Simply sit and listen.

You may experience a new emotion or glimpse a picture, or you may not discern anything. Don't force it. *Simply sit and listen.* When you feel ready, piece your heart back together on your lap. It will resemble a mosaic, with spaces between the pieces. Use a phrase from the Scripture below or choose a phrase or word from one of the Scriptures above and imagine the words falling, like dew, into the spaces of this broken heart—restoring it, mending it, filling it with a love that never ends.

When you are finished with your meditation, you may want to save the pieces of this heart in an envelope to get out at a later time as a reminder of the ways God is working in your life to bring healing and restoration.

> The Spirit of the Lord GOD is upon me,
> because the LORD has anointed me
> to bring good tidings to the afflicted;
> he has sent me to bind up the brokenhearted,
> to proclaim liberty to the captives,
> and the opening of the prison to those who are bound;
> to proclaim the year of the Lord's favor,
> and the day of vengeance of our God;
> to comfort all who mourn;
> to grant to those who mourn in Zion—
> to give them a garland instead of ashes,
> the oil of gladness instead of mourning,
> the mantle of praise instead of a faint spirit;
> that they may be called oaks of righteousness,
> the planting of the LORD, that he may be glorified. (Isaiah 61:1-3, RSV)

2

Living the Questions

Has the Lord rejected me forever?
Will he never again be kind to me?
Is his unfailing love gone forever?
Have his promises permanently failed?
Has God forgotten to be gracious?
Has he slammed the door on his compassion?
—Psalm 77:7-9, NLT

Why me? is one of the existential questions we tend to ask when the bottom drops out of our lives. Parents of children with disabilities and chronic illness often struggle with an additional question: *Why my child?* Although these may be common questions in times of great stress, the questions themselves can bring up feelings of guilt and shame in those who walk a path of faith: *What does it say about my faith if I am questioning God?*

I think the reason I love the book of Psalms so much is because the psalms are full of this lament. They reassure us that it's okay to ask the big questions: *Is God a loving, personal God who cares about the difficulties we face as parents of children with special needs, or a God who set the world in motion at the beginning of time and then stepped away from the action? Is disability part of God's plan? Did God cause our child's disability? Is this some kind of divine punishment?*

We often stifle these questions, afraid of raising God's ire or simply afraid of the pain they cause when we sit with them. When we cram them into the closets of our hearts, the deep emotions surrounding the questions fester, unable to heal. But as we *live* the questions, as we wrestle with God as Jacob wrestled with the angel until the break of day (Genesis 32:24-32), we are often blessed, as Jacob was blessed, with a new name, a new way of looking at our situation, a new way of being—even as we walk with a limp.

ALYSIA is the mother of seven. Her second-born son, Carle, is on the autism spectrum. Her youngest, Jesse, has Down syndrome. Not only does Alysia have seven children, two of whom have significant disabilities, but she also homeschools and partners with her husband as a stateside missionary for HCJB Global, a nonprofit mission organization that spreads the good news of Jesus around the world through radio technology.

I'm sitting on the couch in the family room, the only warm room in the house on this cold October day. (Thank God for electric baseboard heat!) The furnace is broken, and I am curled up under an afghan as I dial Alysia's number. As a youth group leader, I mentored Alysia through her middle and high school years, and we have remained in contact for the twenty-some years since she's graduated.

Alysia is one of the most joy-filled people I know. Our phone conversations always bubble over with laughter even as we move into deep territory.

"I have a story I'd like to share with you," she says after we've caught up on family news. I take a sip of tea and settle in to listen.

"It was Christmastime, and Carle was in his first Christmas play at church. It was a few years ago—he was seven or eight—and he wanted to be an angel, like his sister Betsy the year before. But this particular year they weren't doing a traditional manger scene. It was a Main Street setting, an old-timey feel, kids dressed in hats and scarves, caroling and all of that." She pauses. "Looking back, I wish I would have thought outside of the box. Carle really wanted to be an angel. If I'd thought creatively, I would have asked if he could just stand next to the manger that was on the corner of the stage. But Carle is good at singing, and he's good at memorizing, so I figured it would work out okay." She laughs.

She goes on to tell me that the rehearsals went pretty smoothly, and it looked as if Carle would do fine. The play involved at least thirty children, so the church was packed the night of the performance.

The only problem was the rehearsal hadn't included the spotlight.

"So, it's the night of the play, the kids are on stage, and the spotlight comes on. And Carle is utterly transfixed by that spotlight. I mean *transfixed*. And he's in the center of the caroling scene. He just stands there, staring at that spotlight. All the other kids are singing, and Carle reaches for the end of his scarf and pulls it up around his ear, looping it over his head. And he does the same with the other end of the scarf. So he's standing there with his head wrapped up in this scarf, he's staring at the spotlight, and then he starts swaying back and forth. The only way I can describe it? He looked like Stevie Wonder."

"Oh no," I moan, even as a giggle escapes. We both laugh.

"It *was* funny in the moment," Alysia says. "I mean, what else could we do but laugh? Everyone was laughing. And I couldn't intervene. Honestly, it *was* funny. But the reality was, it was hard. It was really, really hard."

There is a silence on the other end of the phone. It's amazing, the thin line between laughter and tears. I sit and wait.

"We went home, and I was standing at the kitchen window. Suddenly I was totally overwhelmed by sadness. I started sobbing. I asked God, 'Do you think so little of me—that I'm such a bad person—that this had to happen in my life? My kid, with all these sensory issues, all these struggles, sticking out like that?'

"And you know what I heard? I heard God say, 'No, Alysia, I think this *much* of you.'"

Again, there is silence on the other end of the line. I wrap my afghan closer around my shoulders. Again, I wait.

"Will God use Carle in my life to refine me? Yes. Did he create Carle to do this? No. I suddenly understood that Carle has an intrinsic value in and of himself. God wants Carle to be who Carle is—it's a gift. It's not about me— it's about Carle needing a family to grow up in where he can be himself.

"I felt so humbled, Kathy—I felt foolish at my self-centeredness. But I felt so peaceful—I felt God's favor on me. And the truth is, no one in our family can imagine life with Carle not being Carle. He's such a joy. I always tell people Carle is the one who makes me laugh the hardest and makes me cry the easiest."

Alysia laughs as she goes on to tell me more stories of Carle being Carle: calling attention (at the grocery story, in a very loud voice) to a "big, ugly pimple" on a man's face; telling a teacher on a visit to his home, "Your house has a real stench! Why is it *so* stinky?"

"Do you remember that blog entry?" she asks. "The one I wrote a year or so after Jesse was born, and I was grieving? I wrote about how I felt this big black line had been drawn—my life before Down syndrome and my life after. My life wasn't exactly easy or uncomplicated, but I was managing. And with Jesse's birth, I just knew I'd be more tired, more overwhelmed. That there would be less of me to go around, that my other kids would be cheated somehow.

"But somewhere along the way, I fell head-over-heels in love with Jesse. I can't even imagine living on the other side of that black line. And the line itself has changed from a thick black line to a shimmering rainbow of colors."

"What a beautiful image," I whisper.

"I can truly say that my life is far more colorful because of Carle and Jesse. None of us with kids with special needs asked for these kids—we wouldn't have planned it this way. There's lots more pain, fear, unknowns, anxiety, spiritual struggling. But the gift along the way? Our lives are so much more colorful. You come to value *that*. I wouldn't change it for anything now. I can't imagine life without them."

Reflection Exercise

Read Psalm 77 in its entirety. Notice the verbs the psalmist uses: *cry*, *seek*, *moan*. He is letting God know exactly how he feels. Then notice the questions he asks God: *Has the Lord rejected me forever? Will he never again be kind to me? Is his unfailing love gone forever? Have his promises permanently failed? Has God forgotten to be gracious? Has he slammed the door on his compassion?* The psalmist is not holding back.

Read verses 11-12 (NLT):

> But then I recall all you have done, O LORD;
> I remember your wonderful deeds of long ago.
> They are constantly in my thoughts.
> I cannot stop thinking about your mighty works.

Here the psalmist shifts from his present troubles to his experience of God in the past. In verses 16-19 (NLT), he remembers specific things the Lord has done for the people of Israel:

> When the Red Sea saw you, O God,
> its waters looked and trembled!
> The sea quaked to its very depths.
> The clouds poured down rain;
> the thunder rumbled in the sky.
> Your arrows of lightning flashed.
> Your thunder roared from the whirlwind;
> the lightning lit up the world!
> The earth trembled and shook.
> Your road led through the sea,
> your pathway through the mighty waters—
> a pathway no one knew was there!

Write your own psalm of lament to God. Address it to the Lord. Let God know how you feel. Don't hold back! Ask those questions you've been holding in your heart, knowing that God can handle whatever you throw toward heaven.

Then do as the writer of Psalm 77 did. Go back and remember the things God has done for you. The times God has rescued you, blessed you, made the way clear for you.

Notice how you feel after writing your psalm. Was it easy to write out the hard questions, or was it difficult? Did you feel better after doing so? Did the segue to writing about the blessings you've received from God feel natural? Contrived? How did you feel after remembering all that the Lord has done for you?

Finally, surrender whatever you are feeling to God.

3

Doing the Grief Work

CLIMBING THE JADE MOUNTAIN
(filling out my son's SSI forms)
The Chinese poets tell us
that to start an impossible journey,
you must begin with small steps,
one foot in front of the other,
on the rock-hard road. There are
no maps. The mountain gleams
in the afternoon sun. The load grows
increasingly heavy. We
are tired, we are thirsty,
and we want to know
how many dusty miles remain?
The mountain is silent.
All the guidebooks are written
in an ancient language
we don't understand.
When night overtakes us,
we lie down in a dry
river bed, with a stone
for a pillow. Morning
draws her curtains.
We begin again.
—Barbara Crooker, *Line Dance*[9]

PARENTS of children with disabilities know what is called chronic grief. We grieve, first, the death of a dream: the dreamed-of child whom we thought of and talked about, whom we conceived and carried and prayed over in the womb for nine months. Some of us carried our dreamed-of children not in our wombs but in our hearts, and after months or years of labor brought home our adopted children, with absolutely no inkling of what lay ahead.

The dreams we grieve are as unique and varied as each of us. One of us dreams of an athletic child. Another dreams of a musician. Still another dreams of a child who will take over the family business or who will live a life of adventure. We may dream of a studious child, a playful child, a creative child.

Parents of children with disabilities and chronic illness cycle in and out of the stages of grief as our children enter into new life stages. As our child enters school, we may experience some of the same feelings we felt at diagnosis. Grief may manifest when a son turns sixteen and should be driving, when a daughter graduates from high school and her peers are going off to college, when it's time for a child to move away from the family home.

One thing we have in common? All of us dream of a healthy child.

According to Elisabeth Kübler-Ross's landmark studies on death, *On Death and Dying*,[10] when we grieve we go through the following stages (not necessarily in this order):

■ *Denial*. Denial gifts us with time to assimilate new information. It takes some time for our minds to digest and make sense of an initial diagnosis. Denial gives us that much-needed time. Denial is unhealthy only when it continues on, paralyzing us and keeping us from seeking early intervention that could help our child grow and thrive.

■ *Anger*. When reality overpowers denial, anger often rears its head. We may feel anger toward the doctor who delivered the baby or toward our spouse for not supporting us in our own grief or for not being involved enough in the care of the child. Our anger may be directed toward God. We may even be angry at our child. Anger may manifest as simmering resentment or outward displays of rage. Again, anger can be a gift if it is used as a motivator for action and positive change.

■ *Guilt.* This is a common emotion, especially for mothers who carried their children through pregnancy. *What did I do wrong? Was it the wine I had with dinner every night before I knew I was pregnant? Did I exercise too much during pregnancy?* A father or mother may wonder, *Is this God's punishment for sins I have committed?*

■ *Bargaining.* This is the "Let's Make a Deal" stage. "Lord, if you heal my child, I will follow you all the days of my life." "If you lead us to the right doctors, I will volunteer at Children's Hospital." If we don't make pacts with God, we may bargain with ourselves. "If I do enough hours of research, I know I can find the cure for this disability." "If I devote myself to being my child's therapist, advocate, counselor, and social worker, I know we can beat this diagnosis."

■ *Depression.* This stage of the cycle often comes later, at that time when we acknowledge that "what might have been" is gone forever but true acceptance is still a ways down the road. Depression manifests itself differently in each person. While one parent may feel lethargic and unable to complete daily tasks with focus, another may plunge into frantic activity to avoid confronting feelings of sadness and despair. Some may sleep too much, and others not enough. Life loses its luster, and activities that were once enjoyable become routine and boring. When depression is extreme or prolonged, medication or counseling (or both) may be warranted.

■ *Acceptance.* When we are able to let go of our old dreams and dream new dreams, we have found a place called acceptance. This is a time of reaching toward what the future holds for our children. Accepting our children just as they are, we see their many gifts as well as their challenges. Having identified, accepted, and integrated our uncomfortable feelings of denial, anger, guilt, and sadness as part and parcel of who we are, we are freed up to work with more focus toward finding the best medical advice, educational settings, and therapies to make our children's lives as full as possible.

When we allow ourselves to experience these feelings without judging them or willing them away, we find ourselves anchored in the beauty of who our children are, as well as in the hope of glory—Christ Jesus—who dwells within them.

I MET Cindi Ferrini, her husband, Joe, and their son, Joey, at a disability conference several years ago. A dynamic and confident woman, Cindi is the author of several books, including *Unexpected Journey* and *Balancing the Active Life*. Cindi and Joe host a weekly radio spot called "Marriage Matters," and they both speak nationally at FamilyLife Weekend to Remember Get-A-Ways. Recently I've had the pleasure of blogging with Cindi at specialneedsparenting.net, an online community for parents of children with special needs. Cindi often writes and speaks on the topic of parenting a child with a disability, so she was the first person who came to mind for this chapter on grieving.

Born in 1981, Joey is the oldest of the three Ferrini children. Joey has moderate to severe intellectual disabilities due to a condition known as pachygyria. Pachygyria is a rare developmental disorder that results from abnormal migration of neurons in the developing brain and nervous system. Symptoms include poor muscle tone and motor function, seizures, developmental delays, and intellectual disabilities.

"Tell me a little about those early years with Joey," I ask Cindi as we settle in for a phone conversation. I am sitting at my desk in the bedroom, looking out over hundreds of acres of cornfields that lie fallow, waiting for spring plowing.

"Well, you know that one of the first things we have to do is go through the stages of grief. There's denial, where you think this can't possibly be happening to me. Both Joe and I were there. It took most of a year to get the actual diagnosis. As an infant, Joey wasn't meeting the developmental milestones, but he was our first baby. We kept making excuses. But we could see it in his eyes, and his head was so big. He had a hard time holding it up, and he would just lay it on the little tray on his highchair. Our pediatrician sent us to a neurologist when Joey was nine months old.

"We both went through periods of anger. Even still, I can be irritated beyond reason at something—like the way Joey shuffles his feet when he walks! We all have moments of anger, but I always say the important thing is not to park there."

I laugh. "I like that expression."

"Yes, I use that a lot. And then there's bargaining. I remember praying, 'God, if you do this, I will do that.' And Joe shared with me at some point that he did the same thing.

"I wouldn't say that either of us ever fell into depression, as such. But we did experience a lot of disappointment and discouragement. It really was the death of a dream. The dream of the son we thought we were going to have. And Joey was our firstborn. I remember my dad saying to Joe, 'Someday Joey is going to be such a blessing to you.' That was true, but Joe wasn't ready to hear that at the time. I wasn't ready either."

"Do you remember a specific story of a time that you were angry or disappointed?" I ask as I watch a flock of starlings swoop over the fields spread out in front of me.

"Yes," Cindi replies immediately. "We knew someone in the community who was a heavy drinker and drug user. His life was a mess. And yet he had three absolutely lovely, talented children. I found myself telling God, 'We've never been drinkers. We don't even smoke! We did everything right. Why Joey? I don't get it, God!' I was mad! I told Joe what I was thinking, and he answered, 'Imagine if Joey were in that family. He would have been lost.'

"I never complained in that way again. Joe was right. Joey *would* have been lost in that family. I'm so thankful God gave him to us. I think that's when I started to embrace and accept this journey we were on. To embrace the new things that we were experiencing."

The phone line is quiet for a moment as Cindi reflects back twenty-some years. "There was also a specific incident that I remember clearly. During those first years, Joe and I prayed together every night that God would heal Joey. One night while we were praying, this feeling rose up in me. I just *knew* that God would heal him that very night. I was *certain* he would heal him, that he already *had* healed him. I believed that when I walked into Joey's room he would sit up in his bed and say, 'Hi, Mom!'

"I went into Joey's bedroom, and, no, he wasn't healed. I remember being so disappointed and discouraged. But that very night I sensed God speak to my heart, 'I'm not going to do the work in the way you're expecting.' And I surrendered. I can only call it humble surrender."

"*Humble surrender*. I like that phrase," I answer quietly. "It sounds like you had quite a God encounter that night. Where have you most often met God along the way?"

"I would say I most encounter him through the moment-to-moment of my days. I often pray, 'I need you *now*, God.' I know he hears my cries and my laughter. He sees my tears. One thing I pray a lot is, 'Please, Lord, don't let me be frustrated. Let me praise you instead.'"

"Sometimes that's hard," I say.

"Yes, it can be, but that's my biggest desire—to turn my disappointment, frustration, and anger into praise. When people ask me about life with Joey, I want to answer with a positive outlook, yet I don't want to give them an unrealistic idea of what our life is like. I want people to know that I have joy in the journey, but the road isn't always smooth. I don't sugarcoat it. I walk closely with the Lord, but my life isn't perfection by any means!"

"What helped you move toward acceptance?" I ask, my human eyes looking at the fields across the street, but the eyes of my heart looking back at our early years with Joel.

"Total surrender," Cindi answers without hesitation. "You know that as well as I do," she says with a laugh. "Psalm 138:8 is one of my life verses: 'The LORD will fulfil his purpose for me; thy steadfast love, O LORD, endures for ever. Do not forsake the work of thy hands' [RSV].

"I started to see that God was using Joey to make me more like Christ. One thing I often say when I'm speaking is, 'God gives us our husbands to smooth off our rough edges, and he gives us our kids to hack off the rest.'"

I laugh out loud. "I'll have to remember that!"

Cindi laughs too. "Seriously though, living with Joey has made his two sisters more sensitive and caring. They are good, kind people because of their brother."

"But some people never get to that point of acceptance," I say. "I can think of several parents I know who are stuck in bitterness. How do we get unstuck?"

"I could have easily been mired in bitterness," Cindi answers after a moment of silence. "There were so many questions: What happened? What went wrong? Was it something I did? These questions aren't answerable. I went through a difficult labor. I asked myself, did that cause the brain damage? Was it from sitting in the hot tub while I was pregnant? I couldn't park there. God knows, even if it was from something I did, that I didn't do it on purpose. I had to move on. I had to pull out of that parking space!"

"What would you recommend to parents just starting out on this journey through grief toward acceptance?"

"One thing that was very helpful for me was to spend time in a creative outlet. I love to sew. When I had the children, I spent hours sewing kids' clothes, drapes, pillows—you name it. I made my daughter's wedding dress! And then, after she was married and moved away from home, I took up watercolors. It was something I'd always wanted to try. I'm a person who likes color and drawing—I'm not an artist! But it gave me something creative to do.

"I would encourage parents to find something that they love to do: a hobby or interest that is theirs alone. Something they do by themselves. I remember a day, years ago, when I was very frustrated with Joey. My husband said, 'Why don't you go out for a whole day? Do whatever you like to do!'

"I went out and had a wonderful day. When I got home, Joe had an emergency at his dental office, so he had to run out. Joey had a major meltdown—hitting and scratching and kicking me. It was awful. But because I'd had that time away, that time of respite, I was able to look at the situation in a different way. I suddenly remembered that Joey had recently started on new meds for his seizures. I called Joe right away and told him to bring home his *Physician's Desk Reference*. Sure enough, the new med Joey was on had side effects that included aggression. I don't know if I would have put the pieces together if I hadn't had that day to myself!"

"God wants us to take care of ourselves," I say as the five o'clock sun shines slant across the fields.

"Yes, I believe he does. There was a time when taking care of Joey was so intense that I gave up going to exercise class. There were more days than not when I couldn't even get to my sewing machine. I asked a friend, 'What if God asks me to give up sewing? It's the one thing I do for *me!*'

"My friend answered, 'I don't think God would ask you to give up what refreshes you.'"

"Do you agree with that?" I ask.

"I think so. But I have seen, in other places of my life, that when God asks something hard of me, and I obey, that he has a plan. You know, God doesn't say 'be thankful' in all circumstances. He says, 'give thanks' in all circumstances [1 Thessalonians 5:18]. This is something I've learned to do. It gets easier the more I do it—it's like exercise. The more we work our muscles, the stronger they get. And our kids give us plenty of opportunity to work out those particular muscles!

"For years, I had to watch my attitude. It's been a tough area for me. It's easy to get frustrated, and I don't hide it. My kids know when I'm frustrated. My husband knows! But the check for me is, *What are you going to do about it, Cindi?* And then I go to the Lord in prayer."

Reflection Exercise

Take time to go for a walk today. As you walk, ponder the stages of grief that you have walked through as you've parented your special child. Where do you find yourself today? Depression? Anger? Acceptance? Are you bargaining with yourself or with God? There is no right or wrong answer here. You are where you are. As you notice the beauty around you on your walk, ponder these questions:

■ Where am I experiencing God today? In times of quiet prayer? As I shoot out arrow prayers in the hustle and bustle of my days? In times of joy? In my tears?

■ What is the desire of my heart?

■ What might the Holy Spirit say to me if I invited God on this walk, and admitted exactly how I'm feeling?

4

Stopping the Guilt Game

Don't be afraid of yourselves! Don't be afraid of all that you are, in your human reality, where God pitches his tent to dwell with you. God is incarnation. God's new name is Emmanuel, God with us: God with your reality. Open yourself to it without fear. Only in the measure you discover yourself will you discover the depths of his love. In the depths of what you are, you will experience that you are not alone. Someone, lovingly and mercifully, has entered into the mystery of your humanity, not as spectator, not as judge, but as someone who loves you, who offers himself to you, who espouses you to free you, save you, and heal you. . . . To stay with you forever, loving you, loving you!
—Jacques Philippe, *Interior Freedom*[11]

Guilt is a common stage of the grieving process experienced by many parents of children with disabilities and chronic illness. This is where we play the "if only" game. *If only I'd called the doctor earlier. If only I'd spent more time in research. If only I had prayed more, drank less, exercised more, been an all-around better person.*

Guilt creates a black hole in the life of the person who allows it free rein. Guilt saps energy from even the smallest daily tasks. It eats away at relationships, leaving them barren of joy. Living with guilt is like living with a monster that sucks your life force dry then licks its lips and comes back for more. I know. Guilt was an uninvited guest in my life for the first five years of Joel's life.

It took over a year of counseling—as well as the power of the Holy Spirit—to break through the ravages of that guilt. Between the two I learned several lessons:

■ We do the best we can with the information we have at the time we have that information.

■ We're human beings, not God. We are not omniscient. We are not perfect. We make mistakes.

■ We stumble and fall often, and it's only by the grace of God that we're able to pick ourselves up again.

■ We're only able to forgive ourselves if we first open ourselves to God's forgiveness.

The final lesson was the hardest to learn but the easiest to live with: accepting God's forgiveness is incredibly freeing.

WITHIN the past eight months, two of Dave's children, both young adults, have been diagnosed with myotonic dystrophy 1 (DM1), a genetic, multisystem disorder that affects the skeletal and smooth muscle systems as well as the eyes, heart, endocrine system, and central nervous system. The average life span of a person with this disease is forty-eight to fifty-five years, with significant physical disability likely by the end of life. Dave's unborn grandchild is most likely affected, and Dave suspects that he himself has a milder form of the disorder, although he has not yet been tested.

It's more than a father can wrap his mind around.

I meet with Dave at the retreat center he runs with his wife, Jody. Personal retreats, writing retreats, individual sessions of spiritual direction, and training in spiritual direction are offered here. The aroma of fresh-brewed coffee greets me as I walk in the door. The rooms are spacious and light-filled; beautiful shades of yellow, blue, and green soothe the eye as well as the spirit. A pastor, poet, jogger, lover of languages, spiritual director, and professor of spiritual direction, one of Dave's ministry goals is to introduce Christian leaders to the contemplative life. This prayer-permeated retreat space reflects that.

We sit in the living room as Dave tells me his family's story. "Muscular dystrophy is a muscle-wasting disease. In his teens, our son, our youngest child, was dangerously underweight—in the one percentile for height and weight. We just knew in our spirits, as parents do, that something was not right."

Dave and his wife began the doctor marathon, only to be told again and again that Jonathan simply needed to eat more.

"It took ten years of wondering—*Why can't anyone help us? Can nobody just look at him and see something is acutely wrong? What's going on?*"

Dave shakes his head. Unbelievably, it took an Urgent Care doctor, examining an infected scratch on Jonathan's arm, to suggest genetic testing.

Upon learning that Jonathan often had trouble releasing his grip when holding an object tightly, the geneticist examined Jonathan's face, feet, hands, and head, and said he believed testing for muscular dystrophy was in order. The tests came back positive for DM1, a more aggressive form of myotonic dystrophy.

At that time, Jonathan's older sister, Carrie, made a decision to get tested as well, as she shared some similar symptoms. She, too, tested positive for the disease, but with a slightly milder expression.

I look at the icons on the mantel as Dave collects his thoughts.

"Now, in light of the disease, I'm navigating guilt, shame, and embarrassment. I find myself asking, *How could we have been so blind? Could we have advocated harder with the doctors? Why didn't we consider genetic testing earlier?*"

Dave shares his frustration with the ways in which he feels he pushed his son, ten years ago, to perform better in school and in sports.

"I look back at Jon's cross-country races, and how I thought if I just stood at the right places along the course and yelled louder, encouraged more, he would do better. Now I know he only has 60 percent lung function. His muscles don't respond like other people's muscles. They tire more quickly because they're not oxygenated properly. He had two strikes against him. Looking back, I realize how *well* he did. How *courageous* he was. Now I have to be reconciled to myself."

"How is that going?" I ask, knowing from personal experience just how difficult that can be.

Dave pauses a moment. "I've largely been able to forgive myself. I'm able to see that this is a picture of us as humans. At the end of the day, we think we have so much knowledge about the other person—but we don't live their lives. We don't know. We look at people unlike us and make judgments in light of so very little knowledge. Yet we all do, in a sense, the very best we can. It's a whole matrix of environment, imprinting from parents, socialization, and personal wiring that come together to produce a person that does things a particular way.

"How can I be so arrogant to think I know what's best for someone else? I've been so humbled by the events of the past several months. There are times when I wince internally as I remember the times when I tried to badger, goad, cajole, and even embarrass my son into action.

"But I've realized I need to let myself off the hook. Just like everyone else, I've been born of the glory and brokenness of my parents, of that matrix of environment and personal wiring. Sometimes I do things right. Sometimes I do things horribly wrong. But I'm learning to have grace for myself, just as I'm wishing I'd had more grace for my son."

"Where has God been meeting you in this journey, Dave?"

"It feels like I'm becoming more human. Dealing with your children's disabilities brings up messy emotions. This, too, is part of God's work in me—to recognize, give room for, and hold these emotions before God. Not for one second desiring to give way to the lie that says if you really loved Jesus, you would never be sad, never mourn, never weep. That's like saying that if you really loved Jesus, you'd never be joyful!"

We both laugh quietly at the absurdity of that thought.

"I'm trying to simply hold the emotions before the Lord. I'm not feeling orphaned, bereft, or abandoned. But I am experiencing walking in deep sorrow and simultaneously with a Presence that before was only abstract. The middle of Psalm 23 has come alive for me."

"What part of the psalm is that?" I ask.

"*Though I walk through the valley of the shadow of death, I will fear no evil . . . thy rod and thy staff they comfort me.* I'm not in green pastures and I'm not at the banquet table right now. I'm in the valley. But I'm not always going to be in that valley."

Again, Dave pauses. "I have this sense of grief and sadness in the presence of God. His presence doesn't diminish the grief, but it gives it a different color. Does that make sense?"

I nod my head. I find I have very few words as I listen to Dave's story. I have to remind myself that it's okay to simply sit and bear witness to the pain he and his family are going through.

I think we are finished with the interview—we've already gone over our time and someone is waiting for Dave in the next room—but he has one more story to tell.

"You know, I remember sobbing in the car with the news that Carrie's baby would probably be born with a severe form of this disorder. She will most likely deliver the baby in the next week or two—two months early.[12] It was a moment of desolation. But I remember also—it wasn't a voice or a thought—it was a deep understanding that God was bearing witness to my tears at that very moment, that God felt my pain; that he understood the suffering with me, in the car, right at that moment. I remember thinking, *Mark this place. Remember this place where God met you. A stone of witness. Mark it, because you'll be back here again. Mark it as a sacred space where God met you.*"

Again, I find myself at a loss for words. I thank Dave for his time and for the story he's shared.

"It's been a deeply humbling experience," he answers. "I hope it's grown me in compassion and mercy."

Reflection Exercise

Find a comfortable place to sit where you know you will not be interrupted. Close your eyes and take a few deep breaths. Breathe from your belly. When you are relaxed, let your mind take you to a time and place where you experienced the Lord's very real presence. It may have been in childhood, in adolescence, or just yesterday.

Bring the picture of that place up in your mind's eye. See the colors. Reach out and touch something. What do you smell? Allow yourself to relive your meeting with God. Let the feelings resurface. Sit with the Lord for a few moments. Talk to God or sit in silence with the Spirit. Let God's love wash over you. When you have spent enough time, construct a stone of witness in your mind, something to come back to again and again when feelings of shame or guilt threaten to overwhelm you. Remember the love. Remember the love.

SECTION TWO

Embracing Our Brokenness

On July 4, 1999, a twenty-minute maelstrom of hurricane-force winds took down twenty million trees across the Boundary Waters [a million acres of pristine wilderness along the Minnesota-Ontario border]. A month later, when I made my annual pilgrimage up north, I was heartbroken by the ruin and wondered whether I wanted to return. And yet on each visit since, I have been astonished to see how nature uses devastation to stimulate new growth, slowly but persistently healing her own wounds.

Wholeness does not mean perfection: it means embracing brokenness as an integral part of life. Knowing this gives me hope that human wholeness—mine, yours, ours—need not be a utopian dream, if we can use devastation as a seedbed for new life.

—Parker Palmer, *A Hidden Wholeness: The Journey toward an Undivided Life*[13]

5

The Upside-Down Nature
of the Kingdom

The world is broken. We are broken, whether it is through our distractive, fragmented lives or war. Taking that which is broken and creating something whole is an act of healing and restoration. Call it reconstruction.
—Terry Tempest Williams[14]

"Blessed are the poor in spirit, for theirs is the kingdom of heaven" (Matthew 5:3, NIV). These words spoken by Jesus in the Sermon on the Mount form the beginning of Jesus' teaching on life in the kingdom of God. The word "poor" in this first beatitude echoes the word used by the prophet Isaiah, whose prophetic vision found fulfillment in the ministry of Jesus: "The Spirit of the Sovereign LORD is on me, because the LORD has anointed me to preach good news to the poor. He has sent me to bind up the brokenhearted, to proclaim freedom for the captives and release from darkness for the prisoners" (Isaiah 61:1, NIV).

While we tend to think of poverty solely in terms of finances, the concept reflected in the words of both Isaiah and Jesus is a socioeconomic reality that results in impoverishment—a poverty that encompasses and impacts all aspects of life: physical, emotional, and spiritual. According to Dr. Allen Ross, professor of Old Testament and Hebrew at Beeson Divinity School of Samford University, "The word Isaiah uses describes the people who had been taken into exile. They were of course poor, having their land and possessions ripped away, but they were also afflicted and oppressed, they were powerless and without hope, and they were desperate."[15]

I've never been in exile, but there have been many days in my life as Joel's mom that one or all of these adjectives—*afflicted, oppressed, powerless, without hope, desperate*—could have described my state of mind.

Jesus goes on to preach, "Blessed are they who mourn, for they shall be comforted" (Matthew 5:4, NIV). I can definitely relate to this beatitude. I know what it is to mourn a child's disability. I believe you know what that feels like as well.

The Beatitudes comprise one of the best-loved portions of Scripture. I believe these words speak directly to us as parents of children with disabilities or chronic illness. Our lives have been turned topsy-turvy, and here Jesus is telling us that the kingdom of God is a place where life as we know it has been turned on its head.

I MET my friend Rob through a training course in spiritual direction. Both of us were astonished, at the first meeting of our cohort, to find that five out of the nine people in our group, including our teacher, had children with disabilities. One had lost a child to leukemia. Rob is a pastor, has been married for twenty-eight years, and is the father of three sons and a daughter. His third child, Michael, has a rare genetic disorder called cri du chat syndrome, which causes profound cognitive disabilities. Michael is nineteen. (You will meet Rob's wife, Anne, in chapter 9.)

"I have a story about the upside-down nature of the kingdom of God," Rob tells me as we settle in for a quick morning phone conversation. We were scheduled to talk an hour earlier, but although it is his day off, he was called out of the house on a church emergency and we're late getting started. I have an event to attend at my nephew's college in Louisville, a two-hour drive, and need to leave soon. I would love to sit and listen to Rob talk for hours—not only is he wise and funny, but he sounds like my favorite radio announcer on the local classical music station.

"Go for it," I urge.

"It was fifteen years or so ago. We had put the kids to bed, and my wife, Anne, played this Michael Card song ["When a Window Is a Mirror"] for me about a boy named Albert. Albert shuffles when he walks and can't talk. Michael Card sings about Albert being a window that you can see the world through, but that you can also see yourself reflected in. It's a nice song. Anne and I shed a few tears as we listened, reflecting on our own beloved 'Albert.'

"Then we went to bed. About two seconds after I laid my weary body down on the bed, Michael, who had been sleeping well for an hour and a half, began to moan. His moaning quickly turned to cries and then cries with head banging. Anne and I decided to do a complete twenty-three-point inspection."

I laugh out loud.

"We checked the diaper, the sheets, the temperature of the body and room. We checked his fluid levels and all vital components. His breathing was fine, his stomach seemed okay. We couldn't find a problem. So after everything seemed to check out, we closed the hood and returned to bed. Within five minutes he was at it again. Finally, he seemed to rest. But by 2:00 a.m. he was at it again."

I listen quietly, remembering year after year of sleepless nights with Joel, when Wally would lie on the floor just inside Joel's bedroom door so that Joel couldn't wander the house. He was able to keep Joel in his room that way so the rest of the family could sleep, but Wally got virtually no sleep himself on those nights.

Rob continues his story. "We were both up at various points of the night. Anne put in an hour around 2:00 a.m. A couple of hours later I got up to see what I could do. Michael would settle on my shoulder for a while, but the moment I'd try to put him into bed, he would start right back up again. By 5:25 I'd run out of options and patience. As I held him, he continued to bang his head on my shoulder. I gently placed his little face in my hand and said, '*Michael, stop banging your head!*' For some reason, Anne suddenly appeared."

Aching all over, Rob returned to bed, only to see that it was almost time to get up anyway, so he returned to Michael's room and lay on the floor next to Anne, who was sitting in a chair rocking their son. The two of them began to talk.

Rob's voice deepens as he remembers. "That's when I asked her, 'Anne, do you remember Michael Card's song about Albert? The words of his song have convinced me that Mr. Card never spent a night with Albert.' We laughed. I went on and told her that as I'd tried to go back to bed, I realized my neck hurt, my body ached, and I was pretty upset. I knew my day was going to include listening to others complain about their problems, but no one was going to listen to me. I told her that I felt sorry for myself, and angry. But then I told her I decided I had a choice. I could either get angry and upset or I could laugh. I said to her that I figured laughing was the better option. She agreed.

"I went on, talking about how twelve hours earlier I'd been concerned about buying a new house, and how spending the extra money on a house would make it a lot harder to save for future purchases—college was right around the corner for our oldest, our cars were four and ten years old. I was thinking maybe we ought to stay here for ten more years. We'd go a little crazy but we'd be better prepared for the future.

"But lying on the floor that morning, I told her, 'All I want to do is buy the damn house and move.' We had a good belly laugh. We both knew a new house would have more room and more options for where to go with Michael when he can't sleep.

"You know what Anne said then?"

"What?" I ask.

"'We aren't crazy yet!'" Rob laughs. "I answered her, 'No, no we aren't, but we are close, close enough to see it from here!' Again, we both laughed long and hard."

Rob pauses.

"Anne and I went on talking for another fifteen minutes or so, talking about having never expected to enjoy lying on a wooden floor next to a full diaper pail in the wee hours of the morning after being up most of the night with Michael. We talked about the deep love a man can have for a woman, and a woman for a man. We talked about reconfirming our partnership in this life and reconfirming our devotion to each other."

"That's beautiful, Rob." My voice is thick with unshed tears.

"I am amazed," Rob says, "that Anne and I have a vibrant marriage. I'm amazed what a treasure we have. We've been through so many seasons that have been a struggle. And yet I could lie on that floor next to that diaper pail as the sun came up, and we could laugh together. And it's all by the sweet grace of Jesus."

Reflection Exercise

Aside from the Beatitudes, there is no Scripture that better portrays the up-side-down nature of the kingdom of God than 2 Corinthians 12:9 (NIV): "My grace is sufficient for you, for my power is made perfect in weakness."

Search your kitchen cupboard for a cup that is chipped or cracked. If you can't find one that is chipped, take a paper cup and crush it in your hands. Find a quiet spot to sit for a few moments, even if you have to go into your bedroom or bathroom and lock the door. Hold the cup in your hands. Study the cup. Where or how is it chipped or crushed? Close your eyes and take a few deep, cleansing breaths. Find the chipped or cracked place within yourself. Sit with the feelings that arise. You may feel very sad. You may feel angry or agitated. That's okay. Feelings, even the uncomfortable ones, are a gift from God. Admit to God your powerlessness to "fix" the broken place within yourself.

Now meditate for a moment on the things that you can still do with this broken or crushed cup. Can you still use it to carry water? To bail out a boat? To scoop beans for soup?

Again, go back to the broken place within yourself. How might the Holy Spirit use you in your brokenness?

Finally, ask God to fill your broken places with the power and joy of the Holy Spirit, and then simply sit. You may want to repeat a centering word or phrase, such as "Thank you" or "Fill me, Lord," to keep your mind from wandering. Allow yourself, giver that you are, to simply receive.

6

Imperfection—
Part of God's Plan?

Ring the bells that still can ring,
Forget your perfect offering,
There's a crack in everything,
That's how the light gets in.
—Leonard Cohen, "Anthem"[16]

A creation story in the mystical Jewish tradition of Kabbalah goes something like this: God created the world by filling a sacred vessel with holy light. God poured and poured and poured this light—so much light that the vessel shattered—sending bits and pieces of brokenness all over creation. Each broken piece contained a remnant of the light of God. Our job, as humanity, the story goes, is to bring the pieces back together again—*Tikkun Alam*—to "repair the world."

I love this story's profession that God resides in even the tiniest, most broken pieces of creation. But as a Christian, I believe Jesus is the way in which God brings all of the broken pieces back together again. In Colossians 1:17 (NIV) we read of Jesus, "He is before all things, and in him all things hold together." And, of course, it was his death on the cross that provided our bridge to peace and wholeness.

Our children—those with disabilities and those without—are growing up in a culture that is obsessed with perfection. We want the perfect house, the perfect body, the perfect mate, and perfect children. We want to do everything on our own—with our own intellect, our own physical strength, our own ingenuity and imagination.

But the Scriptures tell us that we are cracked vessels containing God's power and light:

> But this beautiful treasure is contained in us—cracked pots made of earth and clay—so that the transcendent character of this power will be clearly seen as coming from God and not from us. We are cracked and chipped from our afflictions on all sides, but we are not crushed by them. We are bewildered at times, but we do not give in to despair. We are persecuted, but we have not been abandoned. We have been knocked down, but we are not destroyed. (2 Corinthians 4:7-9, VOICE)

HOW do we live as cracked vessels, dripping water everywhere we go? As I meditated on the topic for this chapter, I thought of Thom. Thom is a pastor as well as a gifted writer. He has written several books of prayers and poetry for Iona Press. He is also the father of an adopted son with fetal alcohol syndrome. (You will read his wife, Bonnie's, story in chapter 8.)

I met Thom when I was serving on a pastoral nominating committee, searching for a new pastor for our church. Thom was the pastor we called. I will never forget riding in the van with Thom and Bonnie as the nominating committee showed them around our community. When Bonnie and I discovered that we both had three-year-old sons with intellectual disabilities, we immediately knew we would be good friends. They ended up buying a house around the corner from us, and a friendship was born.

When Teddy was adopted at eighteen months of age, his adoptive mom and dad were aware that he had suffered physical and emotional abuse. What they didn't know was that Teddy had been exposed, in utero, to drugs and alcohol. His erratic behaviors—explosive tantrums erupting into aggression—were a result of fetal alcohol syndrome (FAS). FAS is irreversible frontal lobe brain damage caused by prenatal exposure to alcohol or drugs. The child (and adult) may suffer from intellectual disability, extreme impulsivity, lack of a sense of consequences, irrational thinking, an inability to connect with others, explosive rages, or ADHD.

Thom, as the pastor of a medium-sized church, went to work each day, planning services, writing sermons, leading Bible studies, and shepherding the flock, while at home, Teddy's behaviors grew more and more aggressive. Thom was often called away from work to deal with Teddy's meltdowns, which frequently resulted in ambulance runs to the children's hospital psychiatric unit.

Finally, when Teddy was seven years old, Thom and Bonnie made the heart-wrenching decision to move him to a residential setting where he could receive the highly structured professional care he needed to succeed. Teddy was unable to stay in any placement for more than eighteen months, as residential providers would send him home again when his behaviors improved. At home, without the structure he needed, Teddy's explosive behaviors would erupt again, and a new placement had to be found. It was an exhausting journey for everyone involved.

And then one month before his eighteenth birthday, Teddy was diagnosed with stage four testicular cancer. He would spend nearly a year in treatment. Thom and Bonnie were devastated.

Treatment was brutal, but miraculously Teddy was healed of the cancer. He remains cancer-free today, nearly ten years later. But at the age of twenty, Teddy was moved once again because he was doing "too well" for the particular setting in which he was living. The unthinkable happened within days of the move: Teddy's roommate was found dead in his room. There were no witnesses, but Teddy was accused and spent time in jail waiting through legal proceedings that would declare him incompetent to stand trial. Teddy was never proven guilty, but he was moved to a state-run center for children and young adults with developmental disabilities who have been through the juvenile justice system.

Thom and I meet over a cup of coffee at a local franchise. Although I still see Bonnie regularly, it has been quite some time since Thom and I have sat down to talk. It's been more than twenty years since we first met, and the years with Teddy's psychiatric and physical illnesses have taken a toll on Thom physically. He looks tired. But he is glad to see me and willing to reflect on the brokenness in our world and ways in which God, with our cooperation, repairs that world. This is what Thom does in his writing, in his pastoring, and in his family.

With little preamble, Thom jumps into the heart of the matter.

"In the middle of the legal mess with Teddy, I was pretty well convinced that God had a grudge against me. I had a professional relationship with him—I was still serving a church—but personally, I was dealing with anger, disappointment, and bitterness. I couldn't pray for myself, but I never stopped praying."

"How did you pray?" I asked.

"I used formal, structured prayers. And intercessory prayer. I prayed for others when I walked the dogs—never for myself—but for those I knew needed prayer."

"Did you feel that God had abandoned you?" I ask.

"Yes, there were many days I asked myself, 'Has the Lord rejected me forever? Will he never again be kind to me? Is his unfailing love gone forever? Has he slammed the door on his compassion?'"

"Sounds like the psalms of lament," I say, taking a sip of mint tea.

Tom hesitates for a moment. "Yes. But looking back, I have no doubt that God was present. There were too many people who showed up. And the oasis I found in my devotional reading—Henri Nouwen, Richard J. Foster, Barbara Brown Taylor, along with my annual retreats to The Abbey of Gethsemani—all of that helped me sense God's presence."

"How did you keep working?" I ask. "I can't imagine ministering to a congregation when you were dealing with all of this at home."

Thom laughs ruefully. "I had to. It's how we paid for Teddy's medical care. Hundreds of thousands of dollars' worth. We're still paying those bills. I don't know if we'll ever pay them off. And at times, work was a respite. Maybe that's part of God's grace—when there was chaos at home, I found peace at work. And it worked the other way too—sometimes it was peaceful at home and chaotic at work!"

"What keeps you going?" I ask. "Many people would just lie down and say, 'No more!'"

"Truthfully, when I look at Teddy I see Christ. I wonder, *When Jesus comes back, will he come as a disabled person? As a homeless person?* I think he will come as someone we would least expect."

The two of us sit quietly for a moment, envisioning what Jesus might look like the next time around.

Thom breaks the silence. "Do you know what impresses me most about Ted? It's his great delight in the world around him. Music, food, loud bands, cars, motorcycles—he gets such joy out of all these things. We've done things with him, just to keep him busy, that we probably never would have done with a typical kid. And people respond to him in a gentler way."

"He really keeps you busy," I answer. "You drive to Columbus to see him every Saturday, don't you?"

"Every Saturday for almost seven years." Thom shakes his head. I know what a sacrifice this is for him and Bonnie. It's a ninety-minute drive each way. They spend several hours taking Teddy out and about. Gas alone is expensive, and Ted's need for constant activity and entertainment costs even more.

Thom continues. "You know, he has such a compassionate heart. We were eating lunch at the park one day, and there was a homeless man sitting on a bench near us. Ted ran over and gave him half of his sandwich! This isn't anything new. He had a friend named Justin throughout his school years. Justin had cerebral palsy, was blind, and couldn't get around without his wheelchair. Teddy wanted to buy a van with a wheelchair lift so we could take Justin to all of the places we went on the weekends.

"Ted opened my eyes and made me more sensitive to the brokenness in the world. At the same time, I still struggle with God. You know the book that came out after Mother Teresa's death?[17] About her dark night of the soul? I could have written that book. I still feel that I was called to the ministry for a purpose, but some mornings I get up and ask myself, 'Can I still trust God even when my life is going to hell—when I'm on the cross like Jesus and feel abandoned?'"

"Can you tell me a story of meeting God in the struggle?" I ask, clutching my teacup to warm my hands. It feels as if the world has shrunk down to just me and Thom and this booth in which we sit. The fragrance of mint wafting up from the cup bolsters me.

"We'd been in the psychiatric unit with Ted at Children's Hospital, and there was a Habitat for Humanity build coming up for our church. Teddy was almost eighteen at the time. He had just gotten out of the hospital and wanted to help with that build in the worst way. The nurses had noticed a swollen gland on his neck, so I told him we would make a Saturday morning appointment to get that checked out, and then he could go to the Habitat site with me.

"The doctor checked out the gland on Saturday morning and said it was nothing to worry about. So we went on from there to the Habitat site. We had a great day."

Thom pauses for a moment, looking back. "At 12:30 Sunday morning the doctor called. He said he couldn't sleep, that something wasn't right about that gland. He said to get Ted down to the ER at Children's Hospital first thing in the morning. We did. It was cancer. Stage four testicular cancer. He had cancer from his testicle all the way up to his neck. A mass in his abdomen filled up 60 percent of the cavity. There were fifty nodes in his lungs. The saving grace was that it hadn't spread to his bones or his brain. He was just shy of eighteen."

"Oh, Thom," I whisper, wondering how a parent withstands that kind of diagnosis. Even though I'd walked through much of this time with his wife, Bonnie, I didn't know all the details. I'd had no idea how dire the diagnosis was.

"I believe God spoke to that doctor. And God hooked us up with some amazing people in the hospital. The cancer ward was on the fourth floor, and the psychiatric ward was on the fifth. We had help from one floor to the other."

We sit and talk for a few more minutes, sharing favorite authors. I ask Thom for copies of his latest books, *Pirate Jesus: Poems and Prayers for RCL Lec-*

tionary Year C and *Gobsmacked: Daily Devotions for Advent.*
  In *Pirate Jesus*, I find these words:

> i thirst for someone who
> will gather up my brokenness
> and shape me into your peace
> but find few guides
> in this maddened culture.[18]

  And I imagine that Teddy, in all of his brokenness, has been one of those guides for Thom, just as Joel has been for me.

Reflection Exercise

Have you ever heard the parable of the cracked pot? A gardener fills two pots with water each morning to water his garden. One of the pots is cracked, however, and slowly dribbles its water away by the time it reaches the vegetables. Day after day this happens, until the pot feels utterly useless. When the pot can stand his shame no longer, he cries out to the gardener, "Oh, the disgrace of it! To waste precious water, letting you down, master, never fulfilling the purpose for which you molded me!"

  "Look back along the path," the gardener answers. The pot looks behind him and sees that a profusion of blooming flowers grows along one side of the path.

  "You see," the gardener says, "you have fulfilled your destiny. I knew you had a crack, so I planted these seeds which have taken root and bloomed thanks to the water you slowly release on our walk to the vegetables each morning."

  Take some time today to sit with this parable, and ask yourself these questions:

■ In what ways do you see yourself helping God to repair the world?
■ In what ways do you see your child taking part in God's healing work?
■ Who has guided you in gathering up your brokenness and shaping you into the peace of Jesus?

7

Becoming a Wounded Healer

Nobody escapes being wounded. We all are wounded people, whether physically, emotionally, mentally, or spiritually. The main question is not "How
can we hide our wounds?" so we don't have to be embarrassed but "How
can we put our woundedness in the service of others?" When our wounds
cease to be a source of shame and become a source of healing, we have become wounded healers.
—Henri Nouwen, *Bread for the Journey: A Day Book of Wisdom and Faith*[19]

When Joel was in his late teens, I arrived at a prayer retreat aware of a deep
sadness in my spirit, accompanied by physical exhaustion. We had just sur-
faced from six intense weeks with Joel—a hospitalization for influenza and
a secondary infection of pneumonia two weeks later followed by three
weeks of agitation, aggression, and nights averaging two to three hours of
sleep. The manic behavior was a slap in the face—something we thought Joel
had moved beyond two years earlier thanks to the right medication. My
spirit, exhausted beyond the ability to pray coherently, pleaded with God.
*Where are you in this mess, God? Haven't you heard our prayers? How
much will you require of us?*

As I fussed and fumed under my breath, the words to an old hymn by
Daniel Iverson, "Spirit of the Living God," ran through my mind:

> Spirit of the living God, fall afresh on me;
> Spirit of the living God, fall afresh on me.

Melt me, mold me, fill me, use me.
Spirit of the living God, fall afresh on me.[20]

I walked in the woods, and as I walked I meditated on our life with Joel—considering the so-called whole ball of wax of living with autism and how I was allowing that wax to be shaped by fear, anger, despair, and hopelessness. Finally, I hunkered down in prayer, determined not to get up until I had given the entire ball of wax over to God.

Lord, I cried, *I am ready for the fresh wind of your Spirit. I am ready for the heat of your hands to mold me. Dear Lord, this ball of wax that represents our life with Joel is yours. Do with it what you will.*

"Melt me, mold me, fill me, use me." These words became my centering prayer, repeated over and over until I sank into meditation. My internal agitation ceased as my heartbeat slowed along with my breath. A warm, golden light enveloped my body, filling me with peace.

Suddenly an image arose in my mind's eye. I saw two hands holding a ball of wax. The wax was golden, soft, and malleable. The hands held the wax gently, warming it, softening it. The hands began kneading the wax, making a depression in it, hollowing it out. I noticed that most of the work was done with the thumbs. As I watched, the ball slowly became a bowl. Still the thumbs continued to work the wax. Before my eyes, the bowl became larger and larger. The wax became so thin in places it turned translucent. The same golden light that had enveloped me moments before shone through the bowl, an unspeakably beautiful sight. Still, the thumbs worked the wax, shaping it, enlarging it, hollowing it.

I realized the hands belonged to God. God was hollowing me through this painful situation with Joel. I knew God wasn't causing Joel's brokenness but was making all things work for good. God was shaping me, making more room for the Spirit within me. Divine hands were enlarging the space of my tent so that the Lord might tabernacle within me. God's glory shone through the thin places, places thinned by pain. I was becoming a vessel to hold the waters of the Holy Spirit that I might offer a drink to those who thirst, that I might offer shelter through this hollowed-out bowl I've become.

In her poem *Prayer of the Empty Water Jar,* Macrina Wiederkehr, OSB, speaks to this hollowing-out process:

> Jesus, I come into the warmth of your presence
> knowing that you are
> the very emptiness of God.
> I come before you
> holding the water jar of my life.
> Your eyes meet mine
> and I know what I'd rather not know.
>
> I came to be filled
> but I am already full.
> I am too full
> This is my sickness
> I am full of things
> that crowd out
> your healing presence.
> A holy knowing steals inside my heart
> and I see the painful truth.
> I don't need more
> I need less
> I am too full.
>
> I am full of things that block out
> your golden grace.
> I am smothered by gods of my own creation
> I am lost in the forest of my false self
> I am full of my own opinions and narrow attitudes
> full of fear, resentments, control

full of self-pity, and arrogance.
Slowly this terrible truth
pierces my heart
I am so full there is no room for you.

Contemplatively, and with compassion
you ask me to reach into my water jar.
One by one, Jesus, you enable me
to lift out the things
that are a hindrance to my wholeness.
I take each one to my heart and
I hear you asking me,
"Why is this so important to you?"

Like the murmur of a gentle stream
I hear you calling,
Let go, let go, let go!
I pray with each obstacle
tasting the bitterness and grief
it has caused me.

Finally . . .
I sit with my empty water jar
I hear you whisper,
You have become a space for God
Now there is hope
Now you are ready to be a channel of life.
You have given up your own agenda
There is nothing left but God.[21]

Reflection Exercise

Sit with your hands cupped in front of you on your lap. Imagine that this cup or bowl is the water jar of your life. Ask the Lord to show you what obstacles act as hindrance to your wholeness. It may be fear. It may be anger or resentment. It may be a tendency toward busyness or a need to control every detail.

Ask the Lord to help you let go of these obstacles. As your water jar empties, imagine it filling with the life-giving waters of the Holy Spirit. Allow yourself to hear the sound of water filling the basin in front of you. Feel the cool, wet freshness of the water. Watch as your water jar continues to fill until it overflows. Smell the scent of rain-drenched earth surrounding you.

Finally, taste the life-giving waters of the Holy Spirit, the only water that will truly slake your thirst. Know that you are a vessel made to hold the waters of the Holy Spirit that you might offer a drink to those who thirst, that you might offer shelter through this hollowed-out bowl you've become.

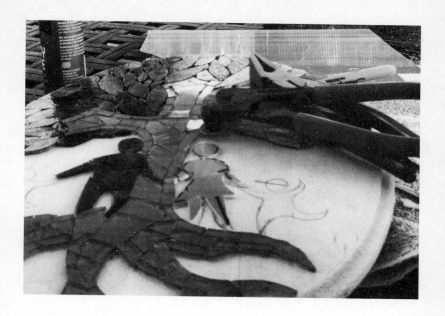

Rearranging the Pieces to Make a New Creation

The journey of faith, the path to spiritual wholeness, lies in our increasingly faithful response to the One whose purpose shapes our path, whose grace redeems our detours, whose power liberates us from the crippling bondages of our previous journey, and whose transforming presence meets us at each turn in our road.

—M. Robert Mulholland Jr., *Invitation to a Journey*[22]

8

The Spiritual Litany of Routine

Are you tired? Worn out? Burned out on religion? Come to me. Get away
with me and you'll recover your life. I'll show you how to take a real rest.
Walk with me and work with me—watch how I do it. Learn the unforced
rhythms of grace.
—Jesus (Matthew 11:28-29, MSG)

In the midst of my grief over Joel's disability, a grief that was intense the first
few years of his life, I searched for God everywhere. One place I found God
without fail was in the uncomplicated rhythms of nature.

No matter how long the day, the quantity or quality of Joel's tantrums, or
the number of doctor and therapy appointments on the calendar, I knew
that, without fail, night would follow day. Joel would go to bed, and, in those
early years, he would sleep. A good book awaited me on the bedside table.
Sleep would knit up "the ravell'd sleave of care"[23] and I would awake the next
morning at least semi-refreshed.

And when Joel was in the midst of a manic phase and no one in the house
could sleep? Without fail the sun would rise, promising a new day, a fresh
slate, a chance to begin again.

It was in the rhythms of nature and the routines of my days that I found
comfort in the midst of anxiety that sometimes verged on panic. I held on to
hope that spring follows winter, year after year, without fail. That beauty
awaited just outside my door.

I found order in the midst of chaos.

BONNIE, whose family's story is told from her husband's perspective in chapter 6, is no stranger to chaos. Teddy was placed with Bonnie and her husband, Thom, when he was eighteen months old, although his adoption was not formalized until he turned three. Teddy's new parents knew up front that their adoptive son had suffered physical and emotional abuse throughout his infancy. But Bonnie was a social worker and her husband was a pastor. They had the resources, and more importantly, the hearts and the faith, to deal with the fallout of abuse. After all, Teddy was still young. And they were flat-out in love with this blond-haired, blue-eyed tyke.

What they didn't know would change the trajectory of their lives beyond imagining. Teddy had fetal alcohol syndrome (FAS). As noted in chapter 6, FAS causes irreversible frontal lobe brain damage that results in a constellation of developmental disabilities that can include explosive rages.

Bonnie and I meet for lunch at a restaurant not far from her home.

"You know that chapter you have planned, 'The Spiritual Litany of Routine'? I want to suggest a new title," Bonnie says, scooping up a steaming forkful of chicken potpie.

I laugh. "Really? Tell me!"

"You'll probably think it's crazy, but as I was looking over your chapter titles, the words just popped into my head. Ready?"

I nod, setting down my soup spoon and picking up my pen.

"'We Should Have Had a Dog from the Beginning.'"

We both laugh.

"Dogs have ministries too," Bonnie says, her eyes bright with memories. "If there is one constant in being a dog owner, it's having to take the dog for a daily walk. Those walks were how we survived."

Conversations swirl around us unheeded during a busy lunch hour, as Bonnie talks to me of two dogs—Cocoa and Dusty—and how the day-in, day-out routine of walking the dogs helped her to bear the unbearable.

Bonnie and Thom's newly adopted son proved to be a highly sociable child with a never-ending grin and energy levels to match. His short attention span meant that Bonnie was on the move constantly as Teddy ran from room to room, house to yard, yard to playground, and playground back home, where the cycle repeated itself until bedtime. A high-energy person herself, Bonnie didn't mind moving from one activity to another. She loved this boy, and she loved being a mother. Her dreams had been fulfilled.

Teddy began exhibiting fits of rage at an early age. His meltdowns were erratic and hard to predict. When he was a toddler, the rages were fairly easy to control, but by the time Teddy was seven, the physical strength unleashed by these electrical surges of the brain was beyond Bonnie's ability to handle. It sometimes took two men to restrain Teddy to keep him from hurting himself or others. By the time Teddy was seven and a half, his parents were searching for residential placements.

The first placement they found was close to home. After an episode of abuse in that setting, they pulled him out. They were shocked to learn that treatment options for children with FAS or mental illness are few and far between. The next closest residential option was a two-hour drive from their home.

Bonnie's heart broke into a million jagged pieces.

Bonnie and Thom made the drive every Saturday to spend the day with Teddy, trying to keep some semblance of normal family life, praying all along to bring him back home again. With structure and professional care, Teddy improved enough over the course of eighteen months to move back home, only to have the explosive behavior erupt again. As a petite woman, Bonnie feared for her life. Another residential facility was located and applied for, with all of the attendant red tape. Again, it was located two hours from Bonnie and Thom's home. Again, they visited Teddy every Saturday. Again, when he showed signs of improvement, he moved back home. Over the course of ten years, this pattern was repeated multiple times.

At the same time, another pattern formed. Cocoa, the dog they had bought for Teddy to love and care for, needed to be walked. Twice daily. Rain, snow, sleet, oppressive heat.

Bonnie asks if I remember the Robin Williams movie *Good Morning, Vietnam*. I nod.

"For a while there, after Teddy was gone, I would open the door, Cocoa on leash, and pronounce in my best Robin Williams impression, 'Good morning, God!' And then we'd take off for our walk.

"It was the only time I could pray, on those walks," Bonnie says. "It was my time to talk to God. The rest of my life was so full of negative things. But that negativity fell away when I walked the dog."

"Why do you think that was?" I ask.

"Well, for one thing, you make connections with people when you're walking a dog. Most people you pass look at you, smile, and say hi. I couldn't help but smile and say hi back.

"I cried a lot—sometimes before, sometimes during, and sometimes after our walks. But when I was done with my mutterings and tears, I was able to get outside of myself. There's a lot to notice when you're walking. I couldn't help but look around and see the wonder of God's creation all around me."

Bonnie lives in a suburban community surrounded by three thousand acres of county park. Towering oaks, maples, beeches, and sycamores provide beauty, shade, and a home to a myriad of birds. Flowering pears line the streets like a white necklace in the spring, and flame maples provide a riot of color in the fall.

Then came the diagnosis of testicular cancer just before Teddy's eighteenth birthday. Friends couldn't help but think of the story of Job. How much suffering could one family take?

And still, the dog needed walking.

"We'd take dog-walking shifts during the cancer surgery and treatments," Bonnie remembers. "No matter how tired we were, it was a wonderful relief after the harsh reality of Children's Hospital. The neighborhood around the hospital is ugly. And scary. Not a good place to walk."

She pauses a moment, the pain of those days etched in her face. "That's when I learned to praise God for all types of weather," she says. "I'd come home and walk the dog, and I was so very conscious that *all* weather was a gift. I didn't even curse him for the sleet," she laughs. "And there *was* sleet in that season."

"What did you pray for on those walks?" I ask.

"I mostly prayed for other people," she answers with a shrug. "Sometimes it felt like my family was beyond God's help, but I never stopped praying for others. Maybe that was the healthiest thing to do at the time. I don't know."

Bonnie tells me how they lost Cocoa just as the cancer debacle was beyond them. Teddy had moved back to his home away from home, and there was some room to breathe again.

One morning Thom called Bonnie from the vet's office. "Cocoa collapsed on our walk today. I don't think he's going to make it. Come as soon as you can."

Bonnie arrived within minutes and held Cocoa in her arms. "You got us through all of this, Cocoa," she whispered. "It's okay. You're okay. You've done your job. You can go now."

We both sit quietly for a moment, Bonnie lost in her memories; my mind filled with pictures of Joel playing on the floor with our beloved lab, Poco, and the day our son Justin sat on the floor with us as we had her put to sleep after major seizures.

"Dogs have ministries too," Bonnie repeats.

Between Cocoa and Dusty, the golden retriever rescue dog that followed, Bonnie's family was to face another huge blow. Teddy was accused of murdering his roommate at a county facility for persons with developmental disabilities. No one saw what happened. It was never proven in court. He was deemed mentally incompetent to stand trial.

How does a parent survive a blow like this?

"The only time I can remember screaming at God was with that murder charge," Bonnie says. "I didn't blame God, but I was so angry."

She pauses. "An elderly woman at our church asked me how I was doing not long after. I told her I couldn't even pray. You know what she said to me?"

I shake my head.

"She said, 'That's why the rest of us are here. So we can pray for you when you can't pray.' Isn't that incredible?"

She shakes her head in amazement as she repeats the words. "'That's why the rest of us are here. So we can pray for you when you can't pray.'"

She goes on to tell me how Dusty loves Teddy, and how the feeling is mutual.

"As soon as we turn the corner to get to Teddy's place, Dusty's head is hanging out the window. And Teddy, who is watching for us, comes barreling out the door, and Dusty races to greet him." Bonnie laughs. "And then he gives Dusty thirty commands in thirty seconds. 'Sit! Stand! Shake hands! Roll over! Play dead!' Poor Dusty!

"Dusty ministers to me and to Thom, but he ministers to Teddy too." Bonnie stares into the space beyond my head. I can tell she's somewhere else.

"It's the closest I've ever come to meditation, walking Cocoa and Dusty. After our walks, I felt I could go on. No, that's not quite right. I *could* go on."

Bonnie and I talked of many other things that day, but looking back, the stories of those two dogs speak loudest. They speak of the litany of routine and how it blesses us when the rest of our life is turned upside down and chaos reigns. They speak of loyalty and unconditional love when the responses of the people around us are less than kind. They speak of a quiet presence and strength mediated through four-legged creatures that wiggle from head to tail when you pick up the leash and head toward the door.

They speak of a love that gets us through.

Reflection Exercise

Find a few minutes today to get outside, no matter the weather. Take a walk, ride a bike, or sit in the yard. Bundle up if it's cold, or grab an umbrella if it's raining. If it's a beautiful day, so much the better!

Ask yourself:

- What daily routines are life-giving to me?
- Which of my daily routines are lifesaving?

■ Where is God in the midst of these routines?
■ What might God be saying to me through these simple rhythms?

End your reflection time with a prayer of thanksgiving, even if it is for something as simple as waking up to a new day each morning or the promise of a good book at the end of the day.

9

Cultivating Gratitude

The quiet song of gratitude, *eucharisteo*, lures humility out of the shadows because to receive a gift the knees must bend humble and the hand must lie vulnerably open and the will must bow to accept whatever the Giver chooses to give.
—Ann Voskamp, *One Thousand Gifts:
A Dare to Live Fully Right Where You Are*[24]

It's four o'clock in the afternoon. I'm sick and exhausted and stressed to the max. Walking into the bedroom, the bed beckons, but the window beyond pulls me like a magnet. The view opens onto several hundred acres of farmland planted each summer in corn or soy. Today, the twelfth of February, fields unfold in winter browns and grays, with undulating rows of corn stubble fading in the distance. The sun shines clear and bright, and clouds hang like ornaments in a blue sky. This is winter's beauty—spare and elegant.

In the distance, I see a flock of turkeys foraging for an early dinner. Suddenly a flock of—how many, a thousand?—starlings lifts off from the field directly in front of me. I'd been so busy staring at the turkeys farther off in the field that I'd looked right past the smaller birds. The flock lifts as one, swooping right, then left, turning and soaring and turning back again in perfectly timed, tightly precise maneuvers. Blue-black wings glint purple in the sun, jewels above the dun-colored field.

I watch for several minutes as the birds lift, soar, and dive bomb the earth, only to head skyward again. Their unison is breathtaking. In one vast turn, they swoop straight toward the house, landing in the century-old maple trees dotting our front yard. After a quick moments' rest, they take off simultaneously for the next field down the road, just out of my line of vision.

My spirit, so downtrodden moments before, lifts; a bubble of joy wells up from the depths. The miraculous flight of this murmuration of starlings (don't you just love that word for a flock of starlings?) plants me in the here and now, opening the ears of my heart to the Spirit's murmur: *Give thanks for this moment—for what is right in front of your eyes.*

I don't know about you, but I too often focus on what lies behind me and what beckons in the future. I so often miss out on the beauty of what's right here right now. How do we learn to cultivate gratitude for the myriad gifts of the Giver? How do we give thanks in the midst of the most difficult of circumstances?

ANNE is the mother of four children. A stay-at-home mom, she is married to Rob, a pastor whose story was told in chapter 5. I've never met Anne in person, but as I listen to Anne's soft voice over the phone, accompanied by a just-under-the-surface laugh and what sounds like a deep-rooted spirituality, I know right away that she could be a close friend, maybe even a soul sister.

Like most parents of children with disabilities, Anne had no contact with disability before the birth of her third child, Michael, who was born with cri du chat syndrome (French for "cry of the cat"). This genetic disorder is characterized by low muscle tone, intellectual disability, low birth weight, slow growth, and slow or incomplete development of motor skills. The name comes from the high-pitched, catlike cry exhibited by these infants.

Michael, at nineteen years of age, is severely affected with low muscle tone. An extremely loving young man, he is a passionate hugger who doesn't know his own strength. Michael is nonverbal and struggles to make his needs known, sometimes becoming aggressive when he can't communicate.

From his birth, it was obvious that something was not quite right with Michael. He was put into the neonatal intensive care unit (NICU) with an

IV immediately after birth because of low blood sugar. However, there was no diagnosis when Anne and Rob left the hospital with Michael when he was five days old. It would take three weeks to receive the results of genetic testing that had been done in the NICU.

"It was such a comfort to take our baby home from the hospital as *Michael*, not as a label," Anne says. "At the same time, I'm grateful that it only took three weeks to get a diagnosis. I know parents who have waited years for a diagnosis."

Anne tells me of three ways she felt the Lord prepared her for Michael's advent into her life. She remembers meditating on 2 Corinthians 1:3-5 in the weeks before Michael was born:

> Praise be to the God and Father of our Lord Jesus Christ, the Father of compassion and the God of all comfort, who comforts us in all our troubles, so that we can comfort those in any trouble with the comfort we ourselves receive from God. For just as we share abundantly in the sufferings of Christ, so also our comfort abounds through Christ. (NIV)

"I was working on memorizing that text, so it was posted on the refrigerator. I came home with Michael, and there it was. I read it with a whole new perspective. It spoke to me of God's sovereignty. I felt him meeting me, right there, right that very moment. I had a new taste of the struggle in my own life that would help me to comfort others. It was profound, really."

Anne is thankful for two other ways in which God prepared her for mothering Michael. While pregnant, she read an article in *Focus on the Family* magazine that spoke lovingly of the life and accomplishments of a boy named Matthew who had Down syndrome. Anne was touched by this positive perspective on a child's disability.

"I remember thinking, *This would be so helpful to a parent of a child with special needs*," she says. "Remembering that article later, I heard God saying, 'I meant for Michael to be in your life, Anne. Michael's a gift.'"

Again, while pregnant with Michael, Anne had heard of someone's struggle in terminating a pregnancy when the baby had been diagnosed, prenatally, with a genetic disorder that would have resulted in severe disability.

"I remember not judging them but saying, 'Wow, I'm going to try to step into their shoes. What would it be like, having to make that kind of decision?' As I prayed with the question, I believed that I would choose to deliver the baby and see how God would walk us through it.

"That was such a confirmation for me. That I would have chosen to have Michael even if I'd known ahead of time what we were facing. I had so much to ponder in my heart."

I look out the kitchen window as I listen. The snow glistens in the sun, and birds crowd around the bird feeder. It's just a few days past Christmas.

"You remind me of Mary," I said, "pondering all those things in her heart."

"You know, a friend of mine said the same thing," Anne says with a laugh. "I've often thought about that. Thought about what Mary tasted—what troubles came to her in that pregnancy, not knowing if people would accept her or reject her. That friend's comment was another confirmation of God being with me. I am so thankful for that."

"You are overflowing with gratitude," I say. "How have you cultivated that discipline?"

Anne hesitates a moment. "Before Michael was born, I had made coasting comfortably through life an art form. I avoided hardship, really. At one point, I recognized my own shallowness and prayed for God to make me a woman of character."

"Be careful what you pray for, right?" I say.

"That's for sure! But really, before Michael I had very little intersection with the disability community. And in the past twenty years this beautiful world has opened to me. I've met the most incredible people—people with a depth of character, a depth of love that I never knew before.

"There was a time when I looked out at everyone else's life and felt discontented, looking past my life at what I was missing. But since Michael I've heard the Lord saying, 'Look at what's in front of you and enjoy it.' That meant my family. Now I'm able to do that—to thank God for what's in front of me right this very minute and see it all as gift."

"It is all gift, isn't it?" I say. "But it's so hard to see it that way when life gets hard."

"Yes, it can be difficult, but choosing to have a thankful heart gives me new energy for my day. I've learned to live one day at a time. I used to cry at the thought of the future. I was insecure at how I'd handle it with Michael's immense needs. I was frightened.

"But I've learned to do the things that Michael wants to do. Look at the ducks in the pond. Watch the birds at the bird feeder. Wonder at the sight of a helium balloon floating up into the sky. It's really good to slow down and be amazed by our world—its sights and sounds—and to be thankful for it all."

"It sounds like you're practicing the presence of God," I reply, thinking of the classic book of the same title.

"Yes. I think Michael's taught me some of what it means to rest in the Lord. You know that verse from Isaiah 30:15? 'In repentance and rest is your salvation, in quietness and trust is your strength, but you would have none of it' [NIV]. Before Michael, I was missing out! I was having none of it! The rest can be an active thing, as we walk forward, learning to trust in God. My soul does find a deeper rest now—a healing rest. I've learned to be okay with not being in constant motion and accomplishment."

Sipping a cup of Moroccan Mint tea as I listen to Anne, I can't help but think of ways in which Joel has taught me the same lesson. So many slow days at the park or in the yard, my eyes opened to the beauty surrounding us.

Anne continues. "To me, practicing God's presence is trusting that he sees me and he sees Michael, and he wants what's good for us. It's so good to expect [God] to be with us, to acknowledge him, and trust him to give us what we need."

"Being known. That's key, isn't it?" I say. "But I know your life is difficult—that Michael's needs are great. Can you tell me a story of struggling with God?"

Anne is quiet for a moment. "The one place I most often find a sacred struggle is in the bathroom with Michael. Every single day starts with toilet and tub time. Rob and I divide and conquer with the team approach, and the morning bathroom time is my job. Daily. Sometimes it's hard. Sometimes I don't want to be there! I find myself praying, quite often, 'Lord, help me see with your eyes—help me see what this can look like so I don't feel so trapped, not wanting to wipe another bottom.'

"And then God grants me an attitude of gratitude. I'm able to say, 'Thank you for Michael.' It lets me go to a place where I can say I'm blessed to have him in my life. That I wouldn't choose to be without him. To know that I won't be in the bathroom all day long. Does that make sense?"

"Yes," I whisper.

"And then I'm strengthened to move through this task of bathing Michael and helping him brush his teeth and dressing him, so that I can consider our relationship instead of an unending task that I have to do."

Anne laughs softly. "Michael loves to run the water—he likes it really hot—and there are many days when I have to say over and over again, 'You have enough water, Michael; enjoy the water you have.' And I shave his face while he plays with a rubber ducky. There is such a paradox in that, isn't there? He's a grown man, really. But we have no idea of how mature he is in his mind."

There is a pregnant pause as Anne gathers her thoughts. "Sometimes I need to step back and say, 'I'm doing this in my own strength. I need you, Lord. I need you. Thank you, Lord. Thank you.'"

Reflection Exercise

In her beautiful book, *One Thousand Gifts: A Dare to Live Fully Right Where You Are*, Ann Voskamp dares herself to make a list of one thousand gifts from God. While Voskamp doesn't have a child with a disability, she does have six children, all of whom she homeschools. She is married to a farmer who works the land they live on. Her life is anything but easy! Her gift list is simple, including things such as morning shadows across the old floors, wind flying cold wild in hair, mail in the mailbox.

Dare yourself to make your own list of simple gifts from God. Keep it next to your kitchen sink. On your desk. Next to your Bible. In your purse or wallet. Each time something beautiful comes to your attention, write it down. Every time you do so, you are making new neural pathways in your brain, muscle memory is growing stronger, and the eyes of your heart are strengthened to see what the Lord is trying to tell you—how very much God loves you and wants to gift you on a moment-by-moment basis.

10

Mindfulness

Oh, my little pork chop, my sweet potato, my tender tot.
You have made me pay attention to the world's smallest
minutia. My pea-shaped heart, red as a stop sign,
swells, fills with the helium of tenderness, thinks it might burst.
—Barbara Crooker, "SIMILE"[25]

Mindfulness. Today's hot topic, we find this word cropping up in newspapers, magazines, and self-help books. It's nothing new, of course. Infants excel in it. Brother Lawrence wrote about it, centuries ago, in *Practicing the Presence of God*. Madeleine L'Engle described it without naming it as moving from *chronos* time to *kairos* time—from human-made time, measured in seconds and centuries—to God's time, where the present moment cradles eternity in its hand.

So what is mindfulness? Jon Kabat-Zinn, founder of the Mindfulness-Based Stress Reduction Program at the University of Massachusetts, describes mindfulness as "paying attention in a particular way; on purpose, in the present moment, and nonjudgmentally."[26]

Poets teach us to cultivate mindfulness. So do children with autism.

Barbara Crooker is an award-winning poet whose poems have been read numerous times by Garrison Keillor on NPR's *Writer's Almanac*. She has nearly eight hundred published poems to her credit, as well as several books, including *Radiance*, *Line Dance*, and *More*. She regularly teaches at writers' workshops, retreats, and conferences.

And yet Barbara describes her main job as caring for her twenty-nine-year-old son, David. Dave has autism.

I had read Barbara's work before I had the privilege of meeting her. She hooked me with her poem "The Mother of a Handicapped Child Dreams of Respite," which I found in her chapbook *Ordinary Life*. The chapbook contains many poems that speak of her life as the mother of a son with autism, but this particular poem was a punch to my gut. I read it out loud to my husband. I read it over the phone to friends. It made me laugh out loud and cry at the same time, so closely did it match my own ambivalence of parenting a son with autism:

> I want to drive away from all of this,
> go clear to California, buzz out on the freeway
> in a white Toyota, put on mirrored sunglasses,
> cut off my hair, feel the hot desert air
> on my bare arms, see a different moon, starker,
> floating in the huge blue ether.
> I will stop when I want to, visit a friend from college,
> drink green tea by a koi pond under wisteria,
> talk until our throats hurt about our complicated lives.[27]

I was so impressed that Barbara had the courage to say what I so often felt but mostly kept bottled up inside, afraid of what others would think if I spoke my truth.

When we finally met at a luncheon for mothers of children with autism, where I was the keynote speaker, I found Barbara to be as delightful as her poetry—no masks, no pretensions, just simply and straightforwardly herself. She was one of the first parents I thought of as I dreamed this book into being.

BARBARA starts out our phone conversation by filling me in on the early years with Dave, the youngest of her three children.

"My children are all seven years apart in age. It wasn't something I'd ever thought about—having a severely disabled son in my later years," Barbara tells me.

"Dave's almost thirty now. He was just fine until his second MMR [measles, mumps, rubella] shot when he was two and a half years old. He went from smiling and lots of eye contact to a blank stare and lining things up. He lost language. We strongly believe his autism is vaccine-related."

We talk for a few minutes about the genetic component of autism, and how measles or rubella, from live vaccines, can live on in the small intestines of those genetically unable to flush them out of the body.

I steer the conversation in a new direction by putting forth the question I've been waiting for weeks to ask. "You know, I'm wondering how mindfulness fits into your life as a poet, and into your life as Dave's mom."

There is silence on the other end of the phone for a moment as Barbara considers the question. "Mindfulness—paying attention to the world around me, the natural world—is part of the religious experience for me. So many people think that experiences of God only take place in a building. Many of us sleepwalk through our lives. We don't even see what's right outside our window. We're all wrapped up in our electronic gadgets instead of paying attention to the sensual world that we experience through our body."

"That's so true," I say, thinking of the kids on the college campus just up the road from our home. How they walk in twos or threes, talking separately on their cell phones, or how they sit with one another in restaurants while furiously pounding out another text, ignoring the friend who is present and certainly missing anything of interest that might be in their path.

"It brings us back to the essentials—the incarnation," Barbara continues, "God made flesh. How much of the body are people aware of anymore? Some of my favorite religious experiences have taken place outside. I have a favorite canvas chair that I take outside to sit and write."

"And Dave taught me to slow down, to pay attention to the smallest things."

"I love your poem 'Autism Poem: The Grid,'" I interject, reading a few lines out loud.

A black and yellow spider hangs motionless in its web,
and my son, who is eleven and doesn't talk, sits
on a patch of grass by the perennial border, watching. . . .
Sometimes he stares through the mesh on a screen.
He loves things that are perforated:
toilet paper, graham crackers, coupons
in magazines, loves the order of tiny holes,
the way boundaries are defined. And real life
is messy and vague. He shrinks back to a stare.[28]

"Yes," Barbara answers. "One of the writing prompts I give my students is this: Look at the world as if you're a camera lens, and focus in on one square inch. Then write what you see."

"What a great exercise! I'll have to try that," I say as I pour a little more honey into my cup of tea. "'Listening to the Mockingbird' is another of my favorites. In it you compare Dave's echolalia [repetition of what's heard] to the song of a mockingbird perched on your chimney. You write of the way Dave can repeat entire dialogues from commercials or TV shows. You end it with the words, 'And all I can do is write it down, write it down.' Do you find the act of looking at that one square inch and writing what you see to be therapeutic?"

"One part of me says no," Barbara answers slowly. "I'm trying to create art. It's an impulse to create something beautiful. On the other hand, the act of writing all those poems on autism *was* enormously healing. I think of the poem 'Diving into the Wreck' by Adrienne Rich. She talks about the engaged life as the life where you're not only facing, but diving into, the wreck of grief. It's painful at times. But going to emotional ground zero is healing."

Barbara pauses again. "You know, I'm not focused on a product. I'm always searching for ways to find the sacred in the details of daily life. It's the writing journey. It's not a contest. It's trying to write that one piece as truly as I can write it. I think of myself as a Zen Lutheran. Mindfulness is at the forefront of my faith *and* my writing. Many poets speak of the Muse as their source of creativity. I give the Muse another name—the Holy Spirit."

"I love that!" I answer. "Speaking of the Holy Spirit, where have you most often met God during this journey with your son?"

"I'd have to say it's often in watching other people interact with him," she says after a moment of silence. "It happens sometimes at the grocery store, or even at church, where not everyone is accepting of someone who is different. I can see that Dave gives people an opportunity to step up to the plate and be kind. It comes when I'm not looking.

"There is one woman I'll never forget. It happened when Dave learned to play the trumpet. Up until the third grade, the school district refused to believe that Dave could be mainstreamed. I never believed he had a low IQ. But they moved him from an educable MR class to a trainable MR class and then to a behavioral unit located in another district. It took a long time of fighting for inclusion before they moved him back to our home district, where he was fully included in a regular classroom with a teacher's aide.

"Dave wanted to play the trumpet, so he took lessons at school and was in the grade school orchestra. There was a mixed-grade concert, with hundreds of kids playing, all ages. The gym was filled. The audience politely applauded when they finished."

Both of us laugh, she at the memory of the cacophony of that concert, me remembering many similar concerts when my boys were in elementary school.

Barbara continues, "After the concert there was a mob scene as everyone tried to find their kids. I saw a teacher from the behavioral classroom coming toward me, swimming against the stream. Tears streamed down her face. When she reached me, she said, 'I am so sorry, Barbara. They completely misjudged Dave's ability to learn.'"

There is silence on the other end of the phone for a moment before Barbara speaks again. "We live in rural Pennsylvania. We belong to a church with a lot of Pennsylvania German reticence. One Sunday some years ago an African American gospel choir came in to lead worship, and they brought a whole entourage with them. The music was glorious, and it was so much fun to hear all of the shouted 'Amens!' and 'Alleluias!' Quite out of the ordinary for our quiet congregation.

"After the service, the choir, along with their family and friends, came through the church and greeted everyone with a handshake. One man came over to greet Dave. I didn't want him to think Dave was rude by not responding, so I said, 'He has a disability and he doesn't talk, but he loved the music.'

"'Jesus loves him anyway,' he responded with a smile before walking on. The heavens opened up. Here was a total stranger giving me what I was looking for as we struggled to find an inclusive school situation for Dave. It was so spontaneous."

As our conversation comes to a close, I am struck by the combination of mindfulness—zeroing in on that one square inch—and spontaneity of which Barbara speaks, and by how our children, along with the Holy Spirit, teach us to value both ways of being.

Reflection Exercise

Today try Barbara's "one square inch" exercise. Take a walk around the house, or if it's a nice day, the yard. Walk until something catches your eye and shimmers with energy. Sit down in front of it, or pick it up and cradle it in your hands. Allow your eyes and your mind to devour every square inch of it. Open up all five senses. Then pretend that your eye is a camera lens. Focus in on one square inch.

What do you see? Describe it on paper or in your mind. How many colors does it hold, or how many shades of the same color? What feelings does it evoke within you? To what can you compare it? Does looking at it bring forth memory? A metaphor?

How does spending time on one square inch of reality impact the way you look at the world throughout the rest of your day? What might God be saying to you through this simple exercise of truly paying attention to the world around you?

11

The Importance of Self-Care

God inhabits our bodies, delighting in every inch of us. Every eccentricity and peculiarity is received. Every longing and self-destructive habit is known. God knows us through and through and still wants to make his home inside of us. The fact that the Holy Spirit wants to abide in us is one way we know how infinitely precious and beloved we are. We are God's own prized possessions. Prized possessions are something you take care of.

—Adele Ahlberg Calhoun,
Spiritual Disciplines Handbook: Practices That Transform Us[29]

The Amplified Bible translates 1 Corinthians 6:19 like this: "Do you not know that your body is the temple (the very sanctuary) of the Holy Spirit Who lives within you, Whom you have received [as a Gift] from God?" How I need to hold on to this truth when I am prone to putting everyone else's needs, particularly the needs of my son, before my own.

Parenting may be one of the most rewarding jobs on earth, but it is also one of the most difficult. Parenting a child with a disability is especially demanding, requiring energy, patience, and perseverance beyond, at times, the humanly possible. As Joel's mom, I have needed God's supernatural power to summon up that kind of energy on a daily basis.

And when I ask God for that Holy Spirit power, God quietly reminds me that the Spirit is available, but I have to cooperate by *taking care of myself.*

When the Pharisees asked Jesus to tell them the greatest commandment, he answered, "'Love the Lord your God with all your heart and with all your soul and with all your mind.' This is the first and greatest commandment. And the second is like it: 'Love your neighbor as yourself'" (Luke 22:37-39, NIV).

I'M GOING to share a little of my own story here. I don't know who you would identify as your "neighbor," but for years, as a stay-at-home mom raising three sons, one of whom has autism, my family was often my "neighbor." Loving them by taking care of them was my primary job.

But I neglected myself. I didn't sleep well; I stayed up late, cramming in books that I couldn't read during the day. I didn't exercise. Who had the time? Healthy foods took a backseat as convenience became the new go-to in the kitchen. I was literally a sugar junkie. Those "trivial" things I loved to do—go to the movies, hang out at the library, have lunch with a friend, read a novel in the afternoon—fell by the wayside as I filled my calendar, determined to be Supermom, Superwife, and Super-Christian.

Even so, in my own mind, I never measured up. I wasn't good enough. Not a good enough mom. Not a good enough wife. Not a good enough daughter or sister or friend. I became physically run-down, catching every bug that came to town. Those things I *did* do to feed my spirit—meditation, volunteering with the youth group, writing—suddenly lost their luster. The world became gray and lifeless as depression descended.

Supermom crashed.

Then one day, in desperate prayer, I cried out to God. "I can't go on like this. I can't live under this kind of stress. It's killing me, physically, emotionally, and spiritually." Out of words, I simply sat, slumped and dejected, repeating my centering prayer: "*Maranatha*; come, Lord Jesus."

Gradually, a deep peace welled up in my chest, flowing like a river through my limbs. I felt heavy and buoyant at the same time—as if I were a deeply rooted tree that had somehow sprouted wings to fly. A golden light shimmered behind my closed eyelids. Out of the silence came a voice—a voice distinctively different from the "you're not enough" voice that had been hounding me for months.

Kathy, I want you to know, down to the deepest part of you, down to your very bones, that you are who I made you to be. Your very footprint was fashioned by me, and in my book are written all the days of your life.

A wave of love nearly knocked me out of my chair. I somehow sat tight, and an image arose in my mind. A picture of my birth certificate rose up, and on it, my miniature footprint, inked on the day of my birth, the one-of-a-kind whorls of my tiny toes and heel clearly marked. And with that sight came the bone-deep knowledge that I was rooted in time and space by that footprint. A footprint fashioned by God.

I am God's beloved daughter. I am enough. I am more than enough.

From that moment on, I was dedicated to taking care of myself, body, mind, and spirit. How did I do that?

First, I tried to spend at least a few minutes every day outside. Simply looking at the sky could bring a prayer of thanks to my lips. Watching the birds at the bird feeder, feeling the wind on my face, letting my bare feet squish in early-morning dew-soaked grass—there was no better way to remember to praise God than to spend time in the world God created, a world that fills all five senses to overflowing.

I began to exercise. Walking was the easiest and most inexpensive form I could find, and a walking trail around a small lake in my neighborhood made that easy.

I made time in my schedule to meet with friends on a regular basis. These were not superficial times of conversation. I sought out friends of the Spirit who listened and shared from the heart, and who loved to laugh as well. My depressed spirit lightened after these times together.

I discovered the little taste of heaven in a simple pedicure. What I'd once disdained as "fru-fru" and ridiculous became one of my favorite once or twice yearly treats. I remember each time someone is rubbing my feet (my husband gives a great foot rub!) that God created these feet. I also think of one of my favorite Scripture texts:

How beautiful on the mountains
are the feet of those who bring good news,
who proclaim peace,
who bring good tidings,
who proclaim salvation,
who say to Zion,
"Your God reigns!" (Isaiah 52:7, NIV)

I wrote down in my journal God sightings—places I'd seen God that day. It was amazing how often, once I started looking, I found God in the midst of even the most difficult days.

I asked my husband to cook more often. He is a fantastic cook, and he was glad to take over in a kitchen I had lost all desire to spend time in. We began eating healthier meals and enjoying food once again. I found myself feeling more energetic than I had in years.

In her book *Sacred Rhythms: Arranging Our Lives for Spiritual Transformation*, Ruth Haley Barton writes about "flesh-and-blood spirituality." In one chapter, "Honoring the Body," she quotes Stephanie Paulsell: "The Christian practice of honoring the body is born of the confidence that our bodies are made in the image of God's own goodness. As the place where the divine presence dwells, our bodies are worthy of care and blessing. . . . It is through our bodies that we participate in God's activity in the world."[30]

As I began to realize this truth—that nurturing my soul also includes honoring my body—moving my own needs up the priority list began to make sense. As I blocked out time on the calendar for myself, my depleted cup began to refill, finally overflowing with more energy for my family, friends, church, and neighbors.

Reflection Exercise

Adele Ahlberg Calhoun writes in *Spiritual Disciplines Handbook*, "The Trinity doesn't call us to overload our bodies and ignore physical symptoms of disease and distress. Rather we are called to recognize body information that can help us make good choices about how to spend our time, grow relationships and nurture our souls."[31] Take some time to journal today, reflecting on the following questions:

■ In what ways do you honor your body and spirit?

■ What is the state of your body? Are you getting enough sleep? Are you eating healthy foods? Do you take time to exercise?

■ What feeds your spirit? What gives you energy—physical, emotional, spiritual? When was the last time you scheduled time on your calendar for these activities?

■ Theologian Howard Thurman writes, "Don't ask what the world needs. Ask what makes you come alive, and go do it. Because what the world needs is people who have come alive."[32] Have a conversation with God about what makes you come alive.

12

Feeding Your Marriage

If we commit ourselves to one person for life this is not, as many people think, a rejection of freedom; rather, it demands the courage to move into all the risks of freedom, and the risk of love which is permanent; into that love which is not possession but participation.
—Madeleine L'Engle, *The Irrational Season*[33]

A family system resembles a mobile—a four-dimensional form of sculpture with freely moving parts. Think of the way mobiles gently sway in the breeze, constantly shifting to find a perfect balance, and you will get an idea of how family systems work.

Family members make up an interdependent system that is ever-changing yet maintains a certain balance, just like a mobile. Each member of the family has his or her own place in the family hierarchy, as well as a distinctive role to play, and family values and rules are implicitly understood. When sudden change occurs, as happens when disability enters the family, the mobile shifts and dances, attempting to maintain its equilibrium and find its former balance.

In a healthy, stable family, family roles are clearly defined and rules are implicitly understood. There is little need for constant renegotiating. But even in the healthiest of families, when disability or chronic illness enters the scene, all the best-laid plans set the mobile to dancing, throwing everything off-kilter. Rules and roles that were taken for granted just yesterday are called into question. A sudden and dramatic shift in the family structure takes place, having a profound impact on the entire system.

One of the first role reorganizations that occurs when a child with a disability or chronic illness enters the family system is that between husband and wife. Dynamics change dramatically as each partner scrambles to find his or her former balance in the system. Taking care of the marriage is of paramount importance in families living with disability if the system is to regain its equilibrium and strength.

I DIDN'T know what to expect the first day of my year-long training course in spiritual direction. As an introvert, stepping into new situations with groups of strangers is difficult for me, but I knew God was on the move and that the people in this group would soon be good friends. I knew without a doubt that I was supposed to be there.

What I never imagined was that five out of the eleven people in our cohort would be parents of kids with disabilities; another grew up with, and ended up caring for, a sibling with autism; another had lost a teenage son to leukemia; and still another was beginning to suspect he himself had a chronic illness. There was no doubt, by the end of our first morning together, that God had gathered this particular group of people together for a very special purpose.

Margo and Glenn, the only spouses within our cohort, are the parents of two young adult daughters. Their youngest, Kristen, was diagnosed with cystic fibrosis (CF) as a newborn. Cystic fibrosis is an inherited chronic disease that affects the lungs and digestive system of about thirty thousand children and adults in the United States. A defective gene and its protein product cause the body to produce unusually thick, sticky mucus that clogs the lungs and leads to life-threatening lung infections.

In the 1950s, few children with CF lived to attend elementary school. Today advances in research and medical treatments have further enhanced and extended life for children and adults with CF. Many people with the disease can now expect to live into their thirties, forties, and beyond.

In the past sixteen months, Kristen has spent 213 days in the hospital. Her lung capacity varies from 30 to 45 percent. A self-sufficient young woman,

Kristen carries the bulk of the weight of communicating with her health care team. Even so, the sheer weight of so many hospitalizations, along with the possibility of a lung transplant in the near future, adds to physical and emotional fatigue not only for Kristen but for Kristen's mother and father as well.

Margo and Glenn have been work partners throughout their marriage as staff members of The Navigators, a ministry of spiritual support for college students. The hallmarks of their ministry are small group studies and one-to-one relationships focused on discipleship. Getting to know this couple over the course of a year, I came to understand why they are so popular among the college kids they serve—they are authentic, warm, caring, fun to be with, and open in sharing both the struggles and joy of their faith walks. It soon became clear that Glenn would supply a good dose of laughter whenever our cohort met, and Margo a generous helping of wisdom.

We meet on the deck at The Springs, the retreat center at which our cohort is meeting. Our chairs overlook the spring-fed lake from which the retreat gets its name.

"I know this has been a difficult walk in many ways, with Kristen's chronic illness," I begin. "I'm wondering where you have most often encountered God along the way."

Margo stares out over the lake for a moment. "The first three years of our marriage, before Kristen was born, Glenn and I were a busy, high-capacity, productive couple—working as partners in The Navigators. After Kristen's birth and diagnosis, life became chaotic and unpredictable. These past twenty-seven years, individually and as a couple, we've made many adjustments in expectations of ourselves and one another as Kristen's needs and frequent hospitalizations have created havoc in our desire to keep going and doing and producing."

She pauses for a moment. "We couldn't have made these adjustments if God hadn't deeply ministered to each of us. Experiencing his care and provision for us financially—and in so many other ways—has given us a big picture of his goodness and sovereignty. Both Glenn and I frequently return to the truth of who God says we are—that we're not 'less valuable' if we're producing less work! Not being able to barrel through life with predictable schedules, energy, and reserves forces this reexamination, and it's a beautiful gift."

"Many of us never learn that truth, that we're valuable just because of who we are, not for what we accomplish," I respond.

"Yes," Margo continues. "Juggling our work, parenting Kristen's older sibling, and supporting a chronically ill daughter—all of this has required unprecedented levels of partnership, give-and-take, and serving one another in our marriage. Apart from the strength, wisdom, and grace of God, I wonder if our marriage would have survived, let alone thrive, as I feel it is today after thirty-one years together."

Glenn nods his head as he listens. "What Kristen's early diagnosis of CF did was vault us into immediate dependence on God. We followed the diagnosing doctor down the hallway and spotted the pamphlets for cystic fibrosis in his back pocket. After he finished walking us through the diagnosis, he calmly said, 'I wouldn't wish this on anyone. I'm sorry.' We were stunned. When the doctor concluded with the sentence, 'Life span averages at twenty-one, but she could live longer,' we were thrust into a whole new arena of trusting God.

"It was a whole new world of experiences, medical terms, medical personnel, and treatments that we never knew existed. But at each of these junctures, we experienced God's calming presence and his healing touch on Kristen's life."

The three of us listen to a mockingbird singing a solo across the lake. Glenn continues. "Now Kristen has miraculously turned twenty-seven. For most of her life, hospitalizations were considered 'tune-ups' and helped stabilize her lung functions. Three years ago we were ushered into a new arena of increased hospitalizations. During the last sixteen months, her hospital visits have totaled over two hundred days."

"Two hundred days—that's over half a year!" I exclaim.

"Yes, it has been a staggering increase from the fifty-day total of two years ago," Glenn answers.

"I can't begin to imagine the grief that would bring up," I say. "Husbands and wives often grieve very differently. How did you—how *do* you—handle those differences?"

Margo and Glenn look at one another. "Sometimes we're like 'good cop/bad cop,'" Margo answers. "One of us will be overcome with sadness and frustration, and the other encouraged and hopeful. We continue to learn to be patient and understanding with one another as we each cycle through various phases of grief—the grief from past losses, current realities, and anticipatory grief as well."

"That's true," Glenn agrees. "We've noticed a pattern over the years. Margo immersed herself in a medical world of knowledge, asking questions and tracking with Kristen's medical team. She began a list of medicines shortly after the diagnosis. Often Margo would be with the doctors, and they would ask her, 'What do you think we should do?' They looked to her as a team member. At that time, I had a difficult time going to see Kristen in the hospital. The majority of my parent time was with our older daughter. Margo would 'schedule' me to visit Kristen in the hospital. It was heartbreaking for me to see her connected to IVs and oxygen."

Glenn is silent for a moment, and again the mockingbird serenades us, this time from the chimney on the retreat house behind us. "Over the years, my heart grieved and often withdrew from the difficulty of the medical situation. As Kristen's health deteriorated, both Margo and I have found new depths of grieving over the losses Kristen has experienced. This past fall, Kristen's health caused me great internal stress. I tried to keep up with life, but I found my emotional responses to be somewhat crippling as we watched our daughter's health slide. We've learned over the years that we tend to allow one of us to deeply grieve and the other to be more involved in Kristen's support. This gives us each a chance to let down emotionally and grieve for the various losses in her life: few friends, not a bright future, not being able to work. We find ourselves trading, with one another, the freedom to grieve."

"That's so important," I say quietly. "To understand that we grieve differently, and to not only allow those differences but to support them as well."

We sit and enjoy the peacefulness of the retreat setting for a moment, watching the springs bubble up from the bottom of the lake, creating concentric circles that move slowly and inexorably outward.

I lean toward Margo. "Tell me a story of a God encounter you've had as a couple on your journey."

"I remember an encounter with God, through a wise friend, early on as we struggled to cope with the new realities of life with Kristen's condition. We were still soldiering on in our work, often giving trite "God-answers" to people's inquiries of 'How are you doing?' This friend sat with us in the hospital cafeteria, looked right at us, and asked, 'What did you *feel* when the doctor told you that?' Even though that was twenty-seven years ago, both Glenn and I remember that moment as a turning point, a time when we realized we were being launched into new territory—meeting God in the midst of raw, confusing, and terrifying emotions."

"Such a simple question—what did you feel—but one most people are afraid to ask!" I reply.

"We've never forgotten it," Margo says.

"I know, from parenting our son Joel, that there is a lot of stress on our marriages as we walk this road with disability and chronic illness," I say to this beautiful couple sitting across from me. "I'm wondering what specific things you have done to strengthen your marriage."

Margo answers first. "Three periods of time in the past twenty-seven years since Kristen's birth we've hit a significant 'wall' in relating well to one another as we carried on our work, responsibilities, and parenting with all the challenges of Kristen's chronic illness. During each of these time periods, we sought out a counselor and spent time together as a couple processing our fears, anger, varying hopes, dashed dreams, and weariness. Thankfully, each of these counseling intensives over the years has given us a way forward and strengthened our marriage."

"Yes," Glenn says. "You know, the types of experiences that couples often have to strengthen a marriage seem to evaporate with a child's chronic health issues. One thing we do is attempt to have communication with each other that does not revolve around Kristen's health. It would be easy to center our conversations around the health regimens, doctor visits, and implications of her cystic fibrosis. Then the core of our relationship would be built on those needed discussions. So we work hard to broaden that communication to ensure that we talk about our faith and new things we are learning.

"We've also attempted to do a few things together that will help us grow spiritually. We attended a quarterly weekend retreat over the span of two and a half years. Margo's family often visited Kristen if she was hospitalized during the time we were away. This past year we've been here at The Springs for two days every other month studying spiritual direction together."

"I'm so thankful God brought us together here!" I respond.

We all agree, and Glenn continues. "These retreats have added deep replenishment as we've learned from the Lord and one another. We also create small diversions in the midst of the reality of Kristen's health. On our thirtieth wedding anniversary, we wound up having dinner away from the hospital cafeteria at a nearby chain restaurant called Moe's. Instead of caving in to the sadness, we talked about how we never dreamed, decades ago, that this is where life would have brought us. And then we received it from the Lord as part of his crafting of our family. Somehow, that dinner became comical instead of depressing.

"We strengthen our marriage by creating pockets of time where we continue to talk and learn from one another. This has resulted in incredible respect and caring for each other along the unpredictable terrain of Kristen's health pathway."

"Has any particular Scripture passage been a comfort and encouragement to you along the way?" I ask.

Margo answers, "Ever since Kristen's birth and diagnosis at two weeks of age, I have clung to Psalm 112:7-8: '[The man who trusts God] does not fear bad news, nor live in dread of what may happen. For he is settled in his mind that [God] will take care of him.' That's from *The Living Bible.*"

"Psalm 34:4 is a meaningful verse to me on seeking God and waiting for his answers," Glenn says, repeating the NIV verse from memory. "'I sought the LORD, and he answered me; he delivered me from all my fears.' We have found that instead of distancing us from God, Kristen's illness has invited us into deeper experiences of trust and love for God."

"Beautiful," I whisper. "This peaceful retreat space reminds me of the importance of creativity and play as we deal with so much day-to-day stress. Hiking in the woods. Walking the labyrinth. Rowing a boat. . ." I point to the rowboat tied to the dock across the way as a perfect word picture of what I mean. "What type of creative outlet, if any, has been a help during the ups and downs of your journey as Kristen's mom and dad?"

Margo answers without hesitation. "Glenn and I have been quite intentional, especially in recent years as the toll of Kristen's declining health adds up, to be stewards of ourselves—to keep identifying life-giving practices, relationships, and pursuits that can help restore depleting energy reserves. I am committed to daily exercise and to carving out periods of solitude weekly or monthly. I give myself freedom to watch sporting events or occasional TV or movies. And I've identified friendships that give me life, and I'm intentional in being with these family members and friends as much as possible."

Glenn sits forward and nods in agreement. "Since Kristen's health has been such a long journey, we've tried to find some ways to keep all of us, as a family, encouraged. We started our creative pathway to alter the pressures we faced by creating a getaway. The first major one, to Disney World and Discovery Cove, was planned for us by the Make-A-Wish foundation. Kristen loved it." He smiles at the memory.

"As her health diminished, fewer options for travel were available. So we periodically went away to a hotel with a pool. Kristen seemed to enjoy the change of pace and getting away from the volumes of medicines that line her room. It was an escape for both her and for us, and a way to pamper the whole family.

"Since her health has deteriorated even more, trips and hotel rooms are becoming a more challenging option. So we've created family nights, where we rent a movie and watch it together. Kristen hasn't been able to go out to movies, especially since her coughing is so pronounced. This has been a fun alternative. With her capacity shrinking to watch a full movie, we have substi-tuted taping some type of sit-com to watch together."

Again, the three of us sit in silence for a few moments before we wrap up our time together and get back to our next session in the retreat house.

Glenn breaks the silence to finish his train of thought and, in so doing, brings beautiful closure to our time together. "So really, what we attempt to do is discern what we 'can do' during this stage of life. We try not to dwell on what we used to be able to do, or what we can't do, and be grateful for what we *can* do together."

Reflection Exercise

In his landmark book, *Anatomy of the Soul*, Curt Thompson, MD, writes about Dr. Daniel Siegel's studies in neuroscience and attachment: "An im-portant part of how people change—not just their experiences, but also their brains—is through the process of telling their stories to an empathic listener. When a person tells her story and is truly heard and understood, both she and the listener undergo actual changes in their brain circuitry. They feel a greater sense of emotional and relational connection, decreased anxiety, and greater awareness of and compassion for others' suffering."[34]

Keeping in mind that sharing our stories leads to transformation, carve out a space of time to spend together with your spouse with the goal of sharing your stories of parenting your child. You may choose to take a long walk in the park, have dinner at a quiet restaurant, or even plan an overnight getaway at a nearby hotel or state park. Take turns telling your stories of ways in which parenting this very special child has impacted your life and faith journey.

When it's your turn to listen, listen deeply. This means no interrupting, no correcting, no fixing. Simply honor your spouse's feelings by listening with every fiber of your being. You may want to use some of the questions from the interview with Margo and Glenn to frame your stories:

■ Husbands and wives often grieve in different ways. How do you grieve? Where do you see yourself in the grief process?

■ Where have you most often encountered God as you've journeyed with your child's disability?

■ Share a story of a God encounter you've had on your journey.

■ Share a story of wrestling with God. How has God met you in that struggle? How has that struggle impacted your faith journey?

■ What Scriptures have comforted and encouraged you along the way?

■ What type of creative outlet, if any, has been a help during the ups and downs of your journey?

When you are finished sharing your stories, close your time together in prayer. You may want to schedule another time to talk about ways in which you have strengthened your marriage along your journey with disability or chronic illness, or ways in which you could strengthen it further.

13

Redefining Success

The only disability in life is a bad attitude.
—Scott Hamilton[35]

In the beginning of my walk with Joel's disability, I devoured every book I could find written by Jean Vanier and Henri Nouwen. Vanier is the founder of the L'Arche communities for people with developmental disabilities. Nouwen, whom I consider to be a mentor and spiritual director (even though we never met in person and he died in 1996), gave up his post at Harvard, with all of its power and prestige, to live as resident priest at Daybreak, one of the L'Arche communities in Canada.

I stumbled upon the writings of Vanier and Nouwen when Joel was a toddler and I was deep into the grieving process. At this stage in my journey, depression was my constant companion. I viewed disability as an enemy to conquer, but I didn't have the energy for the fight. I saw Joel as broken. And we all know that broken things need to be fixed. Yet here were two men of great spiritual insight writing about the gifts men, women, and children with disabilities brought to them personally, as well as to the world as a whole, on a daily basis.

The Holy Spirit whispered a new vision of Joel into my heart as I read.

One of the first quotes from Vanier that I wrote in my journal was this:

> Living with Raphael and Phillippe and many others who have become my brothers and sisters, I began to understand a little better

the message of Jesus and his particular love for the poor in spirit and for the impoverished and weak ones of our society. They have shown me what it is to live simply, to love tenderly, to speak in truth, to pardon, to receive openly, to be humble in weakness, to be confident in difficulties, and to accept handicaps and hardships with love. And, in a mysterious way in their love they have revealed Jesus to me.[36]

Talk about a paradigm shift! In one paragraph, which took me less than a minute to read, I internalized the truth that our basic need as human beings is simply to be loved and cherished for who we are. Not for what we look like. Not for what we accomplish or produce. Not for what we have to give. Our deepest need is to be truly known, and once known, loved and accepted unconditionally. It has nothing to do with power, prestige, or possessions but everything to do with love.

This realization was life-changing. The reverberations still ripple through my life today, a quarter century later, as I come to a bone-deep realization that this is true for me, as well as for Joel. What an affirmation to sit with another mother who has learned, through her beautiful daughter Maria, the same life lessons that Joel has taught me.

KIM and I meet in her home on a blustery day in the middle of October. The kids—she and her husband have four of their own, along with two teenage boys from the inner city who are living with them—are in school, and the house is quiet. Block letters spelling out B-E-L-I-E-V-E take center stage on the fireplace mantel, pillows on the couch send out an invitation to sit back and relax, and the dark day is held at bay by lamplight. We settle in two comfortable chairs facing the picture window. I know Kim doesn't get much quiet time of her own, so we take a few moments to simply sit and breathe.

Kim breaks the silence. "You know, we've never treated Maria any differently than our other kids."

Maria was born with a rare chromosomal disorder called Tetrasomy X, a disorder that causes developmental delays, intellectual disability, changes in muscle tone, and distinctive facial features. Symptoms vary among affected individuals.

Now in her first year of middle school, Maria has two older sisters and a younger brother, and two new brothers who've been a part of the family for nearly two years. Kim tells me how she was on the computer constantly those months after receiving the diagnosis, researching the symptoms, prognosis, and trajectory of the disorder.

"Finally, I had to take my focus off what other people said, what the research said. I couldn't do the support group thing. It was all so negative, hearing the awful reports. That kind of thing puts fear in you, and fear isn't of God."

Kim's phone pings with a text message. She picks it up, looks at it, and puts it back in her pocket. Not only is she mothering six children, but she is a pastor's wife and coaches the girls' basketball team at the local high school. This is one busy woman!

"Some might say we live in denial. We believe in a God who heals and restores. Not necessarily with instant miracles, although I'll never stop believing that God can work in that way. Wait. We *do* live in denial. We choose not to believe in the stereotype of this disorder."

Kim pauses for a moment. I watch the rain out the window as she gathers her thoughts.

"We didn't share the genetic diagnosis with the other kids until a couple of years ago because we didn't want them to treat Maria any differently than they treat each other. We felt like we were going to create a handicap if they were always helping her. We didn't want that."

"Can you tell me a God story in your life with Maria?" I ask.

Kim laughs. "This is my favorite God moment. It happened at a swim meet. We always made our kids be a part of a swim team in the summer, starting at age five. Well, Maria's turn came around, and I knew it would be more difficult for her and more stressful for the coaches. But the coaches worked with her, and by the end of the year she could swim from one end of the pool to the other. And each year there was a new milestone. She was nine before she could swim two lengths of the pool.

"My gut said to take her off the team at that point—the mother in me wanted to shelter her. But we kept on going, and at the end of that summer we showed up at a swim meet. Maria's coach, Mike, who was always very sensitive to her needs, walked up to me and said, 'Kim, tonight's the night for Maria to swim the IM. What do you think?'"

I interrupt. "What's an IM?"

"Individual medley—four lengths of the pool, doing four different strokes. And at this point, Maria could barely swim two lengths. Inside, I was asking, *How dare you even ask?* But I told him to go ask Maria."

I lean forward in my chair. "What did Maria say?"

"Maria said yes, she'd like to try. Her sister Ana was so mad! She thought it was too much to ask. But I told Ana, 'Mike has confidence in your sister. This may be the best day of Maria's life. We have to let her try.'"

By this point, I am totally pulled into the story. Kim's face lights up the dark day, and words tumble out of her mouth.

"The whole swim team and all the parents were gathered around the pool cheering. There were three girls on each end cheering her on, telling her which stroke to switch to. I wasn't even sure she knew the names of the strokes. Everyone else had finished their four lengths by the time Maria finished two, and the fans from the competing team started yelling for her. She did the third length, and she was exhausted, completely past her limit. She paused at the end of the pool, and everyone was yelling 'You can do it! You can do it!' She gritted her teeth and pushed off, and there was a sea of people running down the sides of the pool, urging her on.

"She made it! We had to help her out of the pool because she was so tired, but she was grinning. She'd done it! It was incredible!"

Kim stops for a moment, tears welling up.

"It was a victory not just for her, but for everybody there. Maria is an example *for us* on how to overcome. We always think *we're* supposed to be an example to her of what 'normal' is—but *she's an example to us*!"

We sit in silence for a moment, contemplating the ways in which our kids have so often been teachers not only to us, but to the world around them.

I hate to break the spell, but I have a few more questions. "Are there any particular spiritual disciplines that have helped you, as Maria's mom?" I ask.

Kim nods her head. "Thankfulness has been huge. When you choose to pull yourself out of the world's mind-set, you realize that love is more important than perfection. That helps you look at your kids in a different light. We're a family of athletes—both John and I played college basketball, and all of our kids are drawn to sports. But I am thankful for each one of my kids for who they are, not for what they can or can't do. I'm thankful for the little things—Maria learning to tie her shoes, waking up dry in the morning—the things we so often take for granted. I'm much more thankful now than I used to be."

We talk for a few moments of all of the little things we're thankful for that we used to take for granted. I tell her I'm so grateful that God led us to the church her husband serves—that we have felt within its walls such a welcoming embrace for all of God's children—those with developmental and physical disabilities, those with mental illness and chronic illness.

Kim agrees. "God seems to have put a call on us for ministering to people with disabilities."

As I gather up my purse and book bag to leave, Kim stops me in my tracks. "You know, we decided a long time ago that we wouldn't let this genetic condition define Maria. We wouldn't speak words of disability over her. When she was young, we started speaking blessings over her life—what God would do in her future. We didn't set boundaries around what she could accomplish. And we've seen the fruits of that."

Reflection Exercise

Take a few minutes and sit with Psalm 139:14 (NIV), substituting your child's name: "I praise you because _____ is fearfully and wonderfully made; your works are wonderful, I know that full well."

Notice images of your child that come to mind. You may see her completing a new task, or you may see a beautiful smile that crinkles up his nose. You may remember the way he kissed someone who was hurting or her joy-filled dance when you took her to the park last week. Simply sit and let God reveal your child's giftedness to you. Listen closely to what God reveals to you in this time of quiet. Take a moment and write what you hear or see in your journal.

Tonight, when you tuck your child into bed, speak the words of blessing you heard in your quiet time today over your child. Let her know the many reasons for which you love her. Tell him how much God loves him, exactly as he is.

The Bigger Picture: The Mosaic as Community Art

A mosaic consists of thousands of little stones. Some are blue, some are green, some are yellow, some are gold. When we bring our faces close to the mosaic, we can admire the beauty of each stone. But as we step back from it, we can see that all these little stones reveal to us a beautiful picture, telling a story none of these stones can tell by itself.

That is what our life in community is about. Each of us is like a little stone, but together we reveal the face of God to the world. Nobody can say: "I make God visible." But others who see us together can say: "They make God visible." Community is where humility and glory touch.

—Henri Nouwen, *Bread for the Journey: A Day Book of Wisdom and Faith*[37]

14

Transformed by Invitation

For my house shall be a house of prayer for all nations.
—Isaiah 56:7, NIV

I've spent a lot of time during the last twenty-eight years thinking about invitations or, more truthfully, lack of invitations, for my son Joel. Even the church forgets he loves invitations as much as the next guy. Joel is often excluded because of the outward manifestations of his disability—he can't read, he has a difficult time concentrating, he doesn't do a very good job at sitting still, and keeping his hands to himself can be an issue at times. His differences make some people uncomfortable. He simply doesn't come gift-wrapped in a nice, neat package.

Like most parents of children with special needs, I grieve when Joel is overlooked, ignored, and sometimes rejected. When Joel was five, my grief was too deep to even attempt to knock down attitudinal barriers that kept our behaviorally challenged son from participating in Sunday school and our family from worshipping together. It was easier to leave a church that we loved than try to change it from within. We simply packed up and left, finding a church with an established special needs program.

When Joel was ten, I discovered the newly published book *That All May Worship: An Interfaith Welcome to People with Disabilities*, coauthored and edited by Ginny Thornburgh for the National Organization on Disability. I could barely contain my excitement. Here, in concise and powerful language, was an affirmation of my belief that God's house is meant to be open to *all* people.

As God's creations, we are fashioned uniquely,
Each endowed with individuality of body, mind and spirit
To worship freely the One who has given us life.

Each of us has abilities; each seeks fulfillment and wholeness
Each of us has disabilities, each knows isolation and
   incompleteness.

Seeking shelter from the vulnerability we all share,
Claiming our promised place in God's Household of Faith,
We are transformed by invitation, affirmation and love.

In grateful response, we . . .

Worship and serve God, the source of hope and joy;
Celebrate and serve one another, rejoicing in our diversity;
Transform and serve the world, until we become a Community
which reflects God's Oneness and Peace.

Let the House of God be open to all who would enter
   and worship.[38]

"Yes!" my soul shouted. "Yes! This is it! This is the truth I've known but didn't know how to articulate!"

The words in this book pulled me out of the mire of self-doubt and depression and put wings on my feet, helping me access that place where I stand face-to-face with God and hear the Holy Spirit's truths for my son's life. That place where I hear the invitation called out to Joel and all those children and adults who live with disability, chronic illness, or mental illness.

One of my favorite Scripture texts is the parable of the banquet in the Gospel of Luke. Jesus has a story to tell to a group of Pharisees who have invited him to dinner. The Pharisees haven't invited him out of the goodness of their hearts—they are hoping to trick Jesus into revealing himself as a heretic. The story Jesus tells goes like this: A man once threw a great banquet, sending out invitations to everyone he knew. When the day of the banquet rolled around, he sent his servant out to remind his friends that the party was about to begin. One by one, those he'd invited gave excuses for skipping the festivities. Because the food had been prepared, the wine bought, and the tables set, the host told his servant, "Go into the streets of the city and invite the poor, the maimed, the blind, and the lame." The servant did so, and returned, saying, "Sir, I've found as many people in the streets as I could, but there's still room for more." At that, the host told his servant to go back out to the streets, the back alleys, the fields, and the woods, "and compel people to come in, that my house may be filled" (Luke 14:16-24, paraphrase).

I read this story and know, deep down in my bones, that the ultimate party invitation—an invitation to the kingdom of God—is open to all who will answer the call. I also know, in the deepest recesses of my heart, that Joel will never turn down an invitation made in love.

I MET Ginny Thornburgh in 2009 at an inclusion conference in Katy, Texas. Currently the director of the Interfaith Initiative of the American Association of People with Disabilities, she is also well known for her work in the Religion and Disability Program, which she founded in 1989 at the National Organization on Disability (NOD). A few months earlier Ginny had graciously read my manuscript *Autism & Alleluias*, for which she wrote a cover blurb. To my amazement, this woman whom I held in such high esteem was eager to meet *me*.

To come into Ginny's presence is to feel recognized, known, loved, and appreciated for one's unique, God-given gifts. She emanates a force field of energy that radiates enthusiasm and encouragement. After spending just a short time in Ginny's company, I returned home feeling recharged, recommissioned, and realigned both as Joel's mom and in my writing ministry.

Ginny and I connect again by phone on a sunny Saturday in March. Spring is making a late appearance this year, but the daffodils nod their pretty heads in the breeze, and the fields across the street wait patiently for the farmer's plow. I settle in with a cup of ginger tea. After a few minutes of catching up, Ginny begins our conversation by telling me of her introduction into the world of disability.

In 1963, at the tender age of twenty-three, Ginny met, fell in love with, and married Dick Thornburgh, a "kind, smart, and witty" lawyer from Pittsburgh, Pennsylvania. The father of three sons, Dick had lost his first wife three years earlier in a terrible car accident, a crash that resulted in serious brain injury to his youngest child, Peter. Peter was just four months old at the time, and he spent the next six months in the hospital, where he underwent multiple brain surgeries.

Head over heels in love with Dick, Ginny threw herself into mothering with her characteristic, no-holds-barred enthusiasm. Her energy throws off sparks even over the phone.

"I was a third-grade teacher at the time. I thought to myself, it can't be that hard being a mom! I had no sense in my young brain or soul what it is to be a mom, much less the mother to a child with a disability.

"Dick and the older boys adored Peter. There was lots of teasing, love, and joy in that household. There was little realization for me, at first, of the long-term consequences of Peter's disability. The bigger context for me that first year was 'What's for dinner?'"

We both laugh.

"I gradually began to see that Peter was deeply loved but had not been pushed to do or learn new things. There was no habilitation for him, no saying, 'We know you can do this.' So, on the recommendation of a friend, we went to check out the services offered at what is now The Children's Institute in Pittsburgh, serving children with serious disabilities. And on my twenty-fourth birthday, when Peter was almost four years old, we walked up the steps of this wonderful facility. Peter was the first day student they accepted with a brain injury.

"That's when my education began. OT, PT, speech therapy. The first thing they did was to craft a custom helmet for Peter because he had a portion of the brain with no skull protecting it. The helmet allowed him to be up and running, falling safely, and doing all those things that four-year-olds need to do to grow physically."

In the meantime, when the family attended church each Sunday, the two older boys went to Sunday school while Peter stayed home with a babysitter. Two years later, when Ginny gave birth to a fourth son, Bill, the baby was left at home with the babysitter as well. The family returned to church not long after the birth, and everyone wanted to know when little Bill would be brought in to the nursery. No one asked about Peter.

"It's not as if they didn't know we had Peter," Ginny says. "We were out and about with all four children regularly. All of a sudden, my mind went, *Boing*! I was hurt and angry. What about Peter? Why didn't they ask about Peter?"

The two of us sit in silence for a moment. I watch a squirrel run circles around the maple tree in the front yard while I wait for Ginny to gather her thoughts.

"I went to our minister and director of Christian education and told them, 'This child is my joy. He needs to be here.' And you know what? I met absolutely no resistance.

"Why didn't we do that earlier? I asked myself. We didn't come forward out of shame, laziness, lack of knowledge, confusion—all sorts of reasons. But now I was in mother-bear mode. Soon we had a room assigned to us, and we hired someone to teach the class. We even advertised the class in the local paper. The first Sunday came for the class, and Peter was the only child present! People were so used to being ignored in those years that they couldn't even conceive of a program like this for their children. But I wasn't about to give up.

"With Dick's encouragement, I approached The Children's Institute, and several children who were residents there joined the class. This was the beginning of my work in the field of religion and disability. I can close my eyes now and can see all six of us going to church together each week. Now we were worshipping as a family."

Ginny's calling as an advocate for those who live with disability began at that time, and forty-seven years later she is still going strong.

"Peter, all along, loved everything about faith, Jesus, and the Bible. He was our only son who *wanted* to go to church every week. I read the Bible every morning at breakfast, and when Peter is visiting, he asks me to read it out loud. I'll read a few passages to him and try to get back to my quiet time, and he'll insist, 'Read more! Read more!'

"Because Peter has lived away from us since he was twenty-two or twenty-three, we do a lot of phoning, and once a month he visits us for three or four days. One day I asked him on the phone, 'What's new at church, Peter?' He was quiet for a moment, and then he answered, 'They know my name!'"

"Amazing!" I answer, tears coming to my eyes.

"Yes. That's a pretty deep theological statement, isn't it? And another time, when we were worshipping with him at his church, it came time for the passing of the peace. This is not your typical passing of the peace. People get up and walk all over the church. It's a time to talk and let people know you care about them. Twenty-three people came up to Peter that day. I counted. Twenty-three! Peter looked at me and said, 'This is what church is.'"

"That's incredible," I say. "What wisdom!"

"Yes," Ginny answers. "'This is what church is.' It's the sacred gift of friendship. Once I know your son Joel, and know all about him, and find that he's excluded from an event, I'll say, 'What about Joel? Why isn't Joel here? Is there a reason for that?' When I take time to walk in Joel's shoes, I can anticipate the exclusion and make the event doable for Joel. We want self-advocacy, but it's mighty nice when someone else advocates for us—for our children."

"Yes," I whisper.

"Peter brings so many gifts to us and to his church. His grace, his smile, his laughter and contentment. He slows us down. He changes the whole dynamic. He takes us from frantic to a slower, more thoughtful pace."

Ginny pauses a moment. "You know, it's all been God and Peter. It's nothing we've done. Peter wanted to be confirmed as an adult. He met with his minister five times beforehand. The minister helped Peter write his confession of faith. On the Sunday that he was confirmed, both Dick and I were so anxious when the minister invited us up front with Peter. But Peter stood up, his face grace-filled, confident, and shining."

"What did he say?" I ask.

"'My name is Peter Thornburgh. I am happy in my church. I am happy to have Jesus in my heart.'"

"What a statement of faith," I answer. "Why do we make it so difficult? It's really that simple!"

Ginny has one more story to tell about the uncomplicated yet deep theology held by her son. "I asked Peter once, 'Peter, when you think of God, what words do you think of?' Peter took a deep breath and looked me straight in the eye. Do you know what he answered? 'Nice.' And you know where he learned about that nice God? Through a congregation that loves and cares for him, as well as through his family and friends."

Reflection Exercise

In her foreword to *Amazing Gifts: Stories of Faith, Disability, and Inclusion*,[39] Ginny asks some important questions. Take time to sit with these questions today. If, after answering the questions, you find that your church is missing out on the transformational gifts of people with disabilities (including your own child's unique gifts), you may want to set up a meeting with your pastor or director of Christian education and ask them to go over the questions with you.

Is your church . . .

■ a place where someone like Peter Thornburgh could come to understand God as "nice"?

■ a place where someone who uses a wheelchair, scooter, walker, or cane can easily enter, make friends, worship, and go to the restroom?

■ a place where pain, difficulties, and weakness can be revealed?

■ a place where someone with a long-term mental illness or psychiatric disability is honored and welcomed?

■ a place where an older adult is comfortable suggesting ways to improve lighting and sound systems?

■ a place where no one is ignored and no one is treated as a nuisance or troublemaker?

■ a place where children and adults, with and without disabilities, are included, affirmed, valued, and enjoyed?[40]

15

The Importance of Fellowship

The body of Christ is not something we create. It already is. Paul says, "Because there is one loaf, we, who are many, are one body, for we all share the one loaf" (1 Corinthians 10:17 [NIV]). Sharing our lives with others is always a risk. Authenticity, interdependence and being known come with a cost. But the alternative to paying the cost of living a one-another life is to live cut off from God. By appropriately opening ourselves to each other in the presence of Christ we discover ways to "lay down our lives for our friends." We learn how to become safe people who bring God's welcoming embrace to others.
—Adele Ahlberg Calhoun, *Spiritual Disciplines Handbook*[41]

As the mother of a twenty-eight-year-old son with autism and moderate intellectual disabilities, I often feel bruised and broken. I thank God for friends who surround me with prayer, listen with nonjudgmental ears, and offer emotional support when life veers out of control.

I collect Roseville pottery, a depression-era pottery that was once affordable for the common woman. Grandma Terry gave me my first piece of Roseville—an old-fashioned cookie jar—when I was a young mother. Glazed turquoise green and covered with magnolia blossoms, this cookie jar graced Grandma's kitchen counter throughout my childhood. I remember dragging a chair over to the counter, climbing up, removing the lid, and helping myself to a handful of cookies every time we visited Grandma's house. The lid to the jar is marred by a large chip—probably made fifty or more years ago by me or one of my cousins. Because of that chip, this piece of pottery is much less valuable in the world's eyes but invaluable to me in the memories it conjures.

Many of my Roseville pieces are chipped or cracked—these pieces were more affordable and just as pretty to my eye. Actually, I think the imperfections give them more character. I like to imagine who owned them, what they were used for, what mischievous boy or girl chipped the lip of the vase while filling it with water for a dandelion bouquet.

Over the years, my husband and I have been a part of several small groups. In some of them, everyone's lives seemed so perfect—so free of chips and cracks. As I sat and listened, I couldn't believe anyone else was struggling with the questions that kept me awake at night: Why did God allow my son's disability? Why did God allow suffering? Why was parenting this child so difficult? I found myself unable to share my heart in settings where no one else shared their pain.

What happens in groups where people are willing to be "real" by sharing their broken places? I have found that, little by little, trust builds, and group members begin to see one another as they truly are—not only loved and accepted by God, but valuable in their cracked and weakened state.

Henri Nouwen defines friends who truly care as those who, "instead of giving advice, solutions, or cures, have chosen rather to share our pain and touch our wounds with a warm and tender hand. The friend who can be silent with us in a moment of despair or confusion, who can stay with us in an hour of grief and bereavement, who can tolerate not knowing, not curing, not healing and face with us the reality of our powerlessness, that is a friend who cares."[42]

AFTER years of "knowing" one another through disability ministries over the Internet, Barbara Dittrich and I finally meet up by phone on a Friday morning. After a series of false starts, spring has finally arrived in glorious splendor. I sit at my desk, phone in hand, looking out the window at a world so green it glows. My spirit rises, a tender shoot of new life. How wonderful to start the morning with this view, the scent of new-mown grass, and conversation sprinkled with laughter, encouragement, and talk of God.

The mother of three children, two of whom have significant disabilities, Barb is the founder of Snappin' Ministries, a nationwide support network for parents of children with special needs.

Barb begins our conversation by telling me of the birth of her second child, Charlie, who was diagnosed with hemophilia as a newborn. Barb was no stranger to hemophilia. Her sister's sons had been diagnosed with the disease years before Barb's pregnancy, and Barb, wanting to help her sister in any way she could, had been reading up on the disease and volunteering at the local hemophilia society.

Hemophilia is a rare bleeding disorder in which the blood doesn't clot normally. It is an inherited condition. People with hemophilia have little to no clotting factor, so they bruise and bleed easily, both internally and externally. In severe hemophilia, even minor injuries can result in blood loss lasting days or weeks. The condition can be fatal or permanently debilitating.

Barb remembers sitting in a rocking chair, holding her beautiful baby boy, his soft, fragile skin covered with bruises. "I remember crying, knowing that I passed on these genes. We had gone through years of difficulty to carry a child to term. I'd also gone through years of fertility treatments. I remember asking God, 'Why did you allow this? Did I do something wrong? Were we supposed to adopt? Oh Lord, deliver us!'"

People of deep faith, Barb and her husband prayed, "Thank you, God, for hemophilia. We're not sure why we're thanking you, but we thank you anyway."

In the days ahead, the Dittrich family struggled with countless visits to the hospital, financial burdens, and a lack of support. Researching their son's condition, they found nothing written from a faith perspective. Knowing that God had to be part of the mix if they were going to survive life with this child, Barb sought out another couple of faith for support, a family with a son with multiple physical disabilities. They pursued times to meet to no avail.

Then came a life-changing Bible study called *Experiencing God*.[43] The hallmark of this study is to watch for those places where God is at work and to join the Lord in the midst of that work. As Barb begins talking of the study, my mind flashes back to the Sunday our pastor said, as he held up the *Experiencing God* study guide: "This Bible study is dangerous! Don't proceed unless you are ready to undertake big changes in your life!" I tell Barb that anecdote, with which she agrees wholeheartedly.

"This Bible study didn't leave us where it found us," Barb says with a laugh. "It whacked us over the head. It was as if we heard, 'You fools! It's *you* I want. The Son of Man didn't come to be served, but to serve!' Suddenly, I realized that *we* were to step out—that *we* were to be servant leaders in this world of parenting children with disabilities. We didn't know anything—we were brand-new at this job—but we did know what it's like to walk in these shoes as parents. I often say we were 'dumb obedients'—but that's why God used us! We were willing, but the rest was up to him. The rest is history."

The history Barb refers to is the formation of Snappin' Ministries (www.snappin.org), whose mission is "to support and encourage those living with the daily challenge of parenting a special needs child, so that they may experience the genuine love and hope of Jesus in their everyday lives."

"In 2002 we started out with six couples in our living room, a potluck dinner, and a big box of tissues. I think we had four salads that night—I didn't even know enough to organize the potluck!" Barb laughs again, a hearty, contagious laugh.

That night the gathered people shared their stories. They continued to meet, brainstorming ways to support other parents of children with special needs. The ideas they came up with included providing prayer warriors for each family; sending TLC baskets to those who had just received a diagnosis; building a lending library; finding financial, spiritual, respite, and social resources for families; offering compassion and support; rejoicing with those who rejoice and mourning with those who mourn.

Between the ministry's founding in 2002 and its incorporation in 2007, Barb gave birth to her third child, Sophie. "We knew from the beginning that something was not quite right with Sophie. She had severe allergic reactions to all sorts of things, including the antibiotics prescribed for her frequent ear infections. A dose of penicillin would be fatal at this point."

Sophie has recently, at the age of eleven, been diagnosed with Asperger's syndrome, a mild form of autism.

"Do you feel as if God has used all of this hardship for the good?" I ask.

Barb laughs. "I like to say that God is kind of a pushy dude. Sometimes I wish he'd move along and use someone else!" She laughs uproariously. "Humor is my ultimate coping skill," she says, "along with my faith , of course!"

I can't help but be drawn to this feisty, trailblazer of a woman. I know from reading her blog (www.comfortinthemidstofchaos.com) that life is more than difficult at her home. A simple nosebleed can become a full day's affair in the emergency room, and long, drawn-out IEP (individualized education program) meetings are all-too-frequent occurrences. I think of Henri Nouwen's words in *Life of the Beloved: Spiritual Living in a Secular World*: "Real care means the willingness to help each other in making our brokenness into the gateway to joy."[44]

"There is a healing power in humor," Barb continues. "Someone else might listen to me and say, 'She's one sick puppy!' But I always say, when you can laugh at something, you shrink the size of it. If I can laugh at hemophilia, I'm not a victim of it—laughter takes its power away. When I get together with other parents who are walking this same road and we laugh together, it's empowering."

"That is so true," I say. "I laughed out loud when I read the blog post about your house looking like a crime scene after a particularly bad nosebleed. You said you could spray your house with blood-revealing Luminol and see it glow from outer space."

"Yes, it's a dirty job," Barb says with a laugh.

"You must think that fellowship is important, to have begun this ministry to parents of kids with special needs. Tell me a little more about that."

"No one understands like someone who has walked a mile in our shoes. Nothing gives peace and relief like the compassion we find in journeying together. It's a ministry of presence. There's something in a person's countenance—something unspoken—something in our very presence that is healing."

"I love that," I say, "a ministry of presence."

"Yes. Fellowship is essential. I also call it the 'fellowship of the mat.' Are you familiar with that?"

"No," I answer. "Tell me about it."

"You know the story in the Gospels, where the friends of the paralytic carry him on his mat to Jesus and end up lowering him through the roof because they can't get in the door of the house?"

"Oh yes! I love that story."

"Well, when we're paralyzed by our own circumstances and others usher us into the presence of Jesus, that's the fellowship of the mat. Saint Francis of Assisi said, 'Preach the gospel, and if necessary, use words.' It's our countenance—our presence. When we are simply living our faith, people are attracted to us. Especially when we're under tremendous pressure in our own lives. Others who are suffering look at us and say, 'I want that!' It's that God-shaped hole we're all craving to fill."

"Beautiful," I say. "Tell me a little bit about the mentoring program you've put together for your ministry."

"We started out having local meetings," Barb tells me, "but not everyone could get to them. There's such isolation for some of these parents. We began asking ourselves, 'How can we get to them?' That's when the Snappin' Ministry board began thinking and praying about writing a parent mentor curriculum.

"We had looked at other mentoring programs and found that there was nothing that married the faith piece with the special needs piece. So we put together a group of experts and spent two years developing a curriculum based on best practices in the field and the healing power of the Word of God. It's a twelve-week study, done virtually through Skype, so parents can do it from home. Two of our resources are *Authentic Spiritual Mentoring* by Larry Kreider[45] and Jolene Philo's book, *Different Dream Parenting*,[46] about parenting children and adults with disabilities.

"The program just rolled out in the fall of 2012. We're equipping mentors to come alongside mentees in the right direction. We have six people trained at this time and hope to have several more trained in the near future."

"That's fantastic!" I reply. "How about you? Where do you go for spiritual refreshment?"

"I know I sound like a broken record, but I can't say it enough. Daily time in God's Word is the most important thing. And I journal along with that time in Scripture. It's very therapeutic. I can go back and look at my written prayers, remember what I've been through, and see where I am today. I see who I am in the Lord. And I can say without a doubt that I'm not where I once was because of him."

"Just one more question," I say, sorry to bring the conversation to a close. "Tell me about one God encounter in your life with disability."

Barb is quiet for a moment. I watch a robin dig for worms in the dirt under the maple tree outside my window as she collects her thoughts.

"I'd have to say one of my biggest God encounters came while reading *The Purpose Driven Life: What on Earth Am I Here For?*[47] It was assigned reading for a small group I was in several years ago, with many of the same women who had been in the *Experiencing God* study with me. Rick Warren presents the Word in a fresh, new way in that book. I had been raised by a mother who was mentally unhealthy. She could be very demeaning. I spent a lot of my life regretting who I was because of that. With this book came the realization, 'Oh! God made me who I am so that I can be who he made me to be—to do what he made me to do!'"

I can hear tears in Barb's voice. "Suddenly, the struggles with my kids had *meaning*. That knowledge set me free. I was liberated from all of that regret. God used all those things for the good. He definitely had a plan."

Reflection Exercise

Take a few minutes to pray and journal with the following Scripture:

> Two are better than one, because they have a good reward for their
> toil. For if they fall, one will lift up his fellow. But woe to him who

is alone when he falls and has not another to lift him up! Again, if two lie together, they keep warm, but how can one keep warm alone? And though a man might prevail against one who is alone, two will withstand him—a threefold cord is not quickly broken. (Ecclesiastes 4:9-12, ESV)

Visualize three strands of braided rope. Now imagine someone weaving these ropes together. Visualize the bulk of the new creation. In your mind's eye, see yourself testing its strength with your hands. See yourself using this threefold rope to tie a boat to a dock. Will the rope hold? Do you feel comfortable leaving the boat tied up in any kind of weather?

Now visualize two people you have met on this journey with disability or chronic illness. Perhaps you already meet with them on a regular basis. Perhaps you would like to get to know them better but haven't yet had the time to do so. Imagine the three of you sitting down to talk with one another. Where do you choose to meet? Let yourself be in the scene—notice the colors, the fabric of the chair on which you sit, the fragrance in the air. What part of your story would you choose to tell? Imagine yourself having the freedom to share that story. Visualize the others listening intently, honoring your story by simply listening, without judgment or a tendency to fix. And then see yourself listening as the others share their stories. There may be tears. There may be laughter. Be open to whatever emotions arise.

Again, think of the threefold cord you imagined a few minutes ago. Now imagine your life being bound together with these two other people. What emotions float to the surface? Do you feel a sense of expectancy? Fear in being vulnerable? Freedom in being able to take off your mask? Warmth in their presence? There is no right or wrong answer. Simply notice how you feel. Record your experience in your journal.

16

Putting Together
a Team

One of the marvelous things about community is that it enables us to welcome and help people in a way we couldn't as individuals. When we pool
our strength and share the work and responsibility, we can welcome many
people, even those in deep distress, and perhaps help them find self-confi-
dence and inner healing.
—Jean Vanier, *Community and Growth*[48]

I love the Nigerian proverb "It takes a village to raise a child." In Nigeria, as in
many African countries, children are considered a blessing for the entire community. Older siblings, grandparents, aunts, uncles, cousins, and neighbors
help raise each child to adulthood. Everyone chips in. No one is expected to
go it alone when it comes to parenting.

Here in the United States, families live tucked away in two-, three-, or four-
bedroom homes or apartments. We get in our cars or hop on buses for days
at work, school, and play. At the end of the day, we come home, close our
doors, fix our dinners, watch TV or do homework, and go to bed. Many of
us don't even know our neighbors, much less help raise their children.

"It takes a village to raise a child." What a freeing truth this would be for
parents of children with disabilities or chronic illness. This job simply can't
be done single-handedly. How do we pull together a team that will walk
alongside us? That will help us as we plan for our children's futures?

GAIL WEBSTER is a connector. Twelve years ago, Gail called to share with me a vision for a six-week workshop at her church called "Open Arms." She envisioned gathering together and connecting families of children with disabilities—moms, dads, special-needs kids, and siblings. She also wanted to include people in the congregation who were interested in learning how to make the church a more welcoming space for these families.

The reason for Gail's interest in making the church a place of acceptance? She is the mother of a son, Steven, who has moderate intellectual disabilities. The cause of Steven's brain damage is unknown, but the damage resulted in ongoing seizures when Steven was an infant.

The two of us met and hammered out a six-week plan. After several weeks of advertising the program, we began. Child care was provided for children with special needs, and a special group was formed for siblings, who often play "second banana" to the sib with a disability. The focus of this group was to love, encourage, and have fun with the kids, offering them a safe space to share their feelings about living with a brother or sister with a disability.

The evenings started with a common teaching on how disability affects the family system, and then broke into three groups—a group for moms, a group for dads, and a group for supportive church members. Facilitators led each group, using my book *His Name Is Joel: Searching for God in a Son's Disability*, as a discussion starter.

The workshop was a huge success. Three local churches that sent participants started disability ministries that year, one of which has grown to minister to thousands of people in a yearly special needs prom.

As I said earlier, Gail is a connector.

Gail and I meet for lunch at a local restaurant. It's been two years since we've last seen each other, so we spend some time catching up while we munch on salads and sip hot tea. I'm shocked to learn that Gail's son, Steven—the quiet, unassuming young man with moderate intellectual disabilities I first met twelve years ago—has become a "rock star" in the field of supported employment, not just on a local level, but nationally as well. His business, Steven's Woodshop, has taken him to national conferences where he is known by name. His business, which produces wooden wishing wells as yard orna-ments, has been featured on video and in several newspapers.

I can only shake my head in wonderment as Gail shares Steven's story.

"Tell me how this came about!" I finally find the words to say. "The last time we talked, he had just made his first wishing well and had a job coach a few hours a week! How can other parents find this level of fulfillment for their kids?"

"First," Gail responds without hesitating, "it has to start with prayer. Lots of prayer." Steven is the middle of three children. When all three children were in school Gail became involved in a Moms in Prayer group, a group that prayed for children and teachers in the public school system.

"We prayed for all of our kids," Gail says. "We didn't distinguish Steven as different—he was just one of the kids we prayed for regularly." Gail pauses a moment to take a bite of salad. "One of the women in that group taught me the art of praying ahead. She would regularly ask, 'What's the next milestone Steven is facing that we can pray for?' We were so focused, at home, on the simple day-to-day tasks with Steven—like eating and sleeping and dealing with seizures—that we hadn't thought about praying ahead! I look at where Steven is now and know that God had a plan for him all along. Our prayers were an-swered—every one of them!

"Second," Gail continues, "It's important to have your own social circles. So much of Steven's support comes from my social support system. When he was a baby and things were hard, my friends brought us food and helped us with the house or yard. As he got older, we've regularly had people ask, 'Hey, Steven, would you like to go to the zoo with us today?'

"Connections are key. We fought for inclusion all through school. One of the friendships he made there, with a young woman named Chelsea, has been life-changing for both of them. Chelsea took Steven to the junior prom, and they gradually became good friends. Because of her friendship with Steven, she went on to major in special education in college. She's a special ed teacher today. Yesterday was President's Day, and on her day off school, she and her twin brothers picked up Steven to go bowling. She visits often. She's become a good friend of mine, as well as Steven's."

Gail beams at me across the table, her face radiating joy. "A friend in my prayer group has a son, Chris, who was home from college and needed summer work. A private agency hired him as a job coach for Steven, and he did a fantastic job. He went on to coach several other high school students with special needs.

"When Chris went back to school, and we were looking for a job coach to replace him, another friend from the same prayer group suggested a man she knew from church—a trustworthy fellow who spent his time in retirement volunteering as a handyman at church. She thought he might enjoy working with Steven. It was a great match!

"Network building is the key. It's a long, slow process, but it's key. Get your child as involved as possible. Find an interest he has and pair him with someone with similar interests."

"So how did you pick up on Steven's interest in woodworking?" I ask.

Gail laughs. "Steven always loved to hammer. You know those toy work benches with the colored wooden pegs? I don't know how many of those little wooden hammers and work benches he went through over the years. He hammered for hours. When he was old enough, we let him use a real hammer and nails with a piece of wood.

"His first job coach asked me, 'What does Steven *really* like to do?' I answered, 'He loves to hammer.'

"The next time this fellow came to our house, he brought a pile of wooden bricks. He showed Steven how to nail them into a circle. 'Steven is making a wishing well,' he told me, 'and this is the base.' Steven was so proud of that circle, he brought it into the house."

Soon, Gail tells me, the wishing well was finished, and Steven gave it to her for Mother's Day.

"I wish you could have seen the look on his face," Gail says with a grin. "He was so very proud of himself."

That first wishing well was the beginning of a business venture. The family applied to the ARC for a $2,000 grant for materials and tools: nails, hammers, ear protectors, safety glasses, and other necessities. Steven built four more wishing wells." The Arc is the nation's largest and leading organization for people with I/DD" (Intellectual and Development Disabilities) and their families. His business was featured in two newspaper articles, and business took off. More connections were made, including one with Dave Hammis, the author of *Making Self-Employment Work for People with Disabilities* and *The Job Developer's Handbook: Practical Tactics for Customized Employment.* Hammis's theory is that people's interests, likes, and talents drive what they do successfully, rather than fitting a square peg into a round hole. Hammis received a $1.3 million grant from the federal government, to be distributed within the state of Ohio, to help establish businesses for entrepreneurs with disabilities. Steven got in on this grant and was awarded upward of $20,000 to expand his business—lumber, tools, marketing, brochures, and so on.

"The third thing I recommend people do," Gail goes on to say, "is to get as involved in the community as possible. We've always felt it's important for Steven to do the same things that his brother and sister, or even his dad and I, do. I want as many people as possible to recognize Steven when he's out and about. He knows people at Lowe's now on a first-name basis because of the lumber and tools he buys there. The people at the bank know him by name. He's involved in Special Olympics and in Therapeutic Rec. He belongs to Best Buddies, and we're involved in the Friendship Club for families. Steven volunteers at Matthew 25 Ministries one day a week. He works two hours a week at a local indoor soccer arena, where he runs the vacuum. He also works a few hours a week at a One-Stop Tool Rental business. He loves power washing the big diggers in the yard there. And then, of course, there's his woodshop, located within a local cabinetmaker's shop. He's one of the guys. He feels included and important."

"How about church?" I ask.

"Oh yes. He knows that church is the place where Jesus loves you, because the people there love and accept him. He's in an Open Arms Sunday school class, which is one-on-one. His teachers rotate, so lots of people have come to know him well. He learns about the Bible, and he also cooks in the kitchen.

They make chicken noodle soup to take to people who are sick and chocolate chip cookies to hand out in the adult Sunday school classes. He goes to all the adult functions at church with me and his dad. He's part of our small group—he's an adult now, and he feels a part of things. He brings his photo album with him, and that is his means of communication. People are always looking to see if they 'made the book'! We change the pictures in it on a regular basis, so it's really an overview of his life."

"This is so inspirational, Gail," I say as our meeting time comes to an end.

"It's totally God," she answers, tears in her eyes. "You know, we've always prayed for Steven to reach the potential God has in store for him. And then we gave him all the tools that we could for him to be successful. We equipped him for adulthood, giving him every opportunity to excel at what he's good at.

"Those early years, we grieved. But we've come to see Steven as pure gift. We can thank God today for the brain damage, for making Steven the way he is. He's touched people's lives in a way most kids can't. He's stretched us in so many ways—brought an extra dynamic to our lives that no one else could. He exploded the dynamic! We can't imagine life any differently. We're blessed to live it and share it."

Reflection Exercise

Set aside twenty to thirty minutes to pray and draw a Circle of Support for your child. On a piece of notebook paper, draw four circles, bull's-eye fashion. Label them 1-2-3-4 from the inside out.

1. *Circle of Intimacy.* These are the people whom your child loves and holds dearest. It may be Mom and Dad, brothers or sisters, cousins, Grandma or Grandpa, a best friend or beloved pet. This circle is comprised of people (or animals!) your child chooses to be with because of a deep heart connection.

2. *Circle of Friendship.* This circle is made up of those friends or relatives

your child would choose to go do something fun with but are not necessarily heart connections. They might like to go to the zoo with this person or out to a movie or lunch.

3. *Circle of Participation.* These are the people and/or organizations your child has connections with and where they participate on a regular basis. This circle will include people from church, clubs, work, athletic teams, etc.

4. *Circle of Exchange.* This circle contains people who are paid to be in your child's life: doctors, therapists, teachers, social workers, aides, etc.

In many instances, the circles of support surrounding children with disabilities are filled at the first level—the Circle of Intimacy, and also at the fourth level—the Circle of Exchange—and can be rather bare in the second and third circles—Circle of Friendship and Circle of Participation.

Sit with the Circle of Support you've filled out. Pray about ways in which your child's life could be enriched. Where could your son make connections that would lead him to a more fulfilled life? What are your daughter's interests? Where might she make friends with similar interests? Remember not to compare your child with Steven in the story above or anyone else. Your son or daughter is a unique human being, made in God's image, with a future already planned by God.

At another time, you may feel led to take this one step further and call together a group of people who might journey with you and child in creating a Circle of Support. Consider taking these steps:

■ Check with your county Board of Developmental Disabilities. Facilitators with specialized training can help you with the following process.
■ Decide who to invite. Who, in your own social or family circle, might be interested in walking alongside you and your child as you dream of ways to enlarge your child's world? There may be a teacher or therapist who knows your child well who would be interested in supporting your child in this. But remember, this is a volunteer position, not a paid one!

■ Decide on a location and time to meet.

■ Send out invitations via mail, e-mail, or personal phone call.

■ Set an agenda for the meeting. Two hours is a good time frame. You may be the meeting facilitator, or a person from the Board of Developmental Disabilities may facilitate for you. Here is a suggested agenda from the Indiana Resource Center for Autism:

A. Introduce all circle members. How long has each person known the focus person (facilitator), and how did they meet? Ask other questions that help people get to know one another.

B. Review the individual's life as it is now to build a picture and add to existing information.

C. Clarify ideas about the future. Review obstacles and opportunities, discuss these directions, and select a priority.

D. Record obstacles and opportunities as they arise.

E. Make commitments for action.

F. Set the next meeting time and place.[49]

Tools of the Mosaic Artist:
An Introduction to the Spiritual Disciplines

Practices are the nuclear reactors of the Christian faith, arenas where the gospel and human life come together in energizing, even explosive ways. Practices create openings in our lives where the grace, mercy and presence of God may be made known to us.

—Thomas Long, in a review of Craig Dykstra's
Growing in the Life of Faith[50]

17

Prayer

In simple humility, let our gardener, God, landscape you with the Word, making a salvation-garden of your life.
—James 1:21, MSG

This morning I bring my Bible, journal, and cup of tea into the garden. A light mist hangs over the fields across the road, and I am surprised to see tender green shoots of corn forming rows where yesterday there was nothing but dirt. All around me, Dame's Rocket thrusts purple and white spires toward the skies like holy hands reaching toward heaven. Green boxwood shimmers in the breeze, and a yellow weed at the fence line bursts into flame as a sunbeam peeks through the clouds.

The words of Psalm 63 (RSV), my reading this morning, reverberate through my mind.

> O God, thou art my God, I seek thee,
> my soul thirsts for thee;
> my flesh faints for thee,
> as in a dry and weary land where no water is.
> So I have looked upon thee in the sanctuary,
> beholding thy power, and glory.
> Because thy steadfast love is better than life,
> my lips will praise thee.

So I will bless thee as long as I live;
I will lift up my hands and call on thy name.

In the sanctuary of this garden, the desert landscape of my heart—that dry and dusty place where worry and anxiety about Joel sometimes threaten to overwhelm me—turns to an oasis of green, flowing with streams of living water. Prayer rises up within me as praise.

No wonder poets and songwriters often refer to the garden as a metaphor for prayer.

And yet gardens are not always lush and beautiful. Think of the garden in the midst of drought. Parched plants wilt. Green leaves turn brown. What was abounding in exuberance just weeks before suddenly sags under the weight of cloudless skies with no promise of rain in sight. Nothing will revive a drought-stricken garden like a gentle, soaking rain.

It is no different for the gardens of our hearts. Sometimes, in the words of my son Joel at the end of a major meltdown, "We need Jesus!"

As the mother of a son with autism, I was first drawn more deeply into prayer because of an intense thirst for God's presence. I was desert-thirsty, parched for the living waters Jesus promises in John 4:14 (NIV): "Whoever drinks the water I give them will never thirst. Indeed, the water I give them will become in them a spring of water welling up to eternal life."

I don't know about you, but I often go to prayer because I want to make sense out of something senseless (a beautiful boy with a damaged brain). Because I can't handle the situation on my own (*I don't know how to mother this son, Lord. You are going to have to show me how*). Because I crave peace in the midst of chaos (the roller coaster ride with autism, anxiety, and manic phases is often overwhelming). And the more I spend time with God, the more the garden of my heart blooms with an unquenchable love for the things of the Spirit. I need God's presence just as my garden needs the rain.

THOSE who have spent a lifetime practicing the discipline of prayer tell us that prayer is not only communication with God; it is also about communion with God's Spirit. When we pray, we are invited into a divine intimacy.

Prayer is so much more than the one-sided conversations prompted by our intercessory prayer lists. Prayer is a way of listening to God, of communing with God, of experiencing God's presence within us, of resting in God's presence and truly knowing what it means to be God's beloved child.

In *Celebration of Discipline*, Richard J. Foster writes, "In prayer, real prayer, we begin to think God's thoughts after Him: to desire the things he desires, to love the things He loves. Progressively, we are taught to see things from His point of view."[51] That's intimacy!

Jesus talks about this intimacy in his prayer to the Father when he prays that we may be in him as he is in the Father and the Father is in him (see John 17:20-26).

God invites us into spiritual intimacy, but as is true in many relationships, we are afraid of intimacy. Ever notice how we edge around prayer? The next time you attend a prayer meeting, compare the ratio of time spent talking *about* prayer with the amount of time actually spent *in* prayer. When fifteen minutes are set aside for prayer, we often talk about our prayer requests for twelve minutes, leaving only three minutes at the end to pray.

I think one of the reasons we try to stay on the surface of prayer is that we know, deep down, that, as Foster has written, "to pray is to change."[52] When we offer ourselves to God—not our shopping list of things we desire, not our intercessory prayer list, not our agenda for the day, but *our very selves*—the Holy Spirit begins the transforming work Paul writes about: "Even to this day when Moses is read, a veil covers their hearts. But whenever anyone turns to the Lord, the veil is taken away. Now the Lord is the Spirit, and where the Spirit of the Lord is, there is freedom. And we all, who with unveiled faces contemplate the Lord's glory, are being transformed into his image with everincreasing glory, which comes from the Lord, who is the Spirit" (2 Corinthians 3:15-18, NIV).

Many times our thirst for God leads us into an adventure in prayer—our tried-and-true ways of praying are no longer satisfying. As we grow in intimacy with God, we outgrow old prayer patterns. In *Sacred Rhythms: Arranging Our Lives for Spiritual Transformation*, Ruth Haley Barton writes, "Like a plant that has become pot-bound, its roots searching for nutrients that have long since been used up, the human soul gets to the point when it is ready for a more spacious way to pray, one that provides more room for the mystery of growth in intimacy with God and more depth for the roots to sink into."[53]

We may find that the structured prayers we've depended on since childhood or young adulthood—the Lord's Prayer, litanies, the rosary, and others—leave us hungry for more. We may need to fertilize our roots by soaking in the Lord's presence with a breath prayer consisting of one or two simple words, spoken with every inhalation and exhalation.

Perhaps we've had an intercessory prayer list tucked in the pages of our Bibles for years. One day we wake up to find that we're praying for people we don't even know without the expectancy of seeing a healing. That may be the day we decide to attend a healing prayer service, where we experience hands-on prayer by a prayer team that prays with great expectancy. We may actually witness a miracle or, better yet, experience an emotional or physical healing of our own.

Taking up an intentional prayer practice can grow our relationship with God. For example, the *Prayer of Examen* is a practice of remembrance. In the Daily Examen, we make a commitment each night before going to bed to pray back through our day. The Examen is a discipline of looking at ourselves honestly—the good, bad, and the ugly—and asking God to show us where we fell short as well as remembering the places where God met us throughout our days. We know that God loves us unconditionally, and yet invites us to transformation. We're called to become, with each passing day, more like Christ. Psalm 139:23-24 gives us a model for this type of self-examination: *"Search me, O God, and know my heart; test me and know my thoughts. See if there is any wicked way in me, and lead me in the way everlasting."*

Those of us who come to God with many words might benefit from spending time in *contemplative prayer* or *meditation* (see chapter 18 for more about meditation as a Christian practice). In this form of prayer, we use a centering word or phrase to quiet our minds and focus our attention on God's loving presence: "Maranatha, Come Lord Jesus; The Lord is my shepherd; Thank you; Jesus."

Prayer Imagery is a wonderful avenue for the visual among us. To be guided into the Lord's presence with the imagination can take us to completely new levels of understanding the depths of God's love for us as beloved sons and daughters of the Most High King. The Scriptures, both Old and New Testament, are filled with images that we can easily enter with our imaginations: The Twenty-Third Psalm, Jesus' teaching on the vine and the branches in John 15, and the Parable of the Sower (Mark 13: 1-9) are just three examples. The paper heart used in the reflection exercise of Chapter One of this book, as well as the chipped cup used in Chapter Five are both examples of prayer imagery using a concrete image that we can hold in our hands as we pray. There are many gifted Prayer Imagery practioners who use the imagination and the Scriptures to take us into the Lord's presence (see http://envisionguidedimagery.com/prayer-imagery/in-the-scriptures for one example).

Finally, those of us who have a habit of coming before God with request after request might find that a *prayer of gratitude* transforms our grasping demeanor to a posture of open hands: hands that are ready to receive the many gifts God has to offer. We may pray this prayer as we go to bed each night, looking back over our day for those things for which we are thankful, or we may keep a gratitude journal, jotting down God-sightings throughout our day. With practice, many find that consciously looking for blessings in the midst of difficult or hum-drum days becomes an unconscious habit, transforming our way of looking at the world.

Consistency is another key to developing our prayer lives. It helps to find a special *place* to pray and to use it often. In the living room of my house, we have a comfortable, overstuffed armchair that is dark green and embossed with a leaf pattern. I have spent hundreds, if not thousands, of hours praying in what my husband and I call the prayer chair. Simply sitting in that particular chair brings me into an attitude of prayer.

Consistency in a prayer *time* is helpful as well. While my husband and I have a short time of prayer together most mornings, I like to pray after he has left for work and I have the house to myself. It is much easier to enter the quiet for an extended length of time when there are no distractions. (When the boys were living at home, I took this time after everyone left for school.) If I have early appointments and don't have an opportunity to pray first thing in the morning, there is a good chance that, caught up in daily activities and routines, I will not take the time later in the day. You, however, may be drawn to prayer at the end of the day, when work is done and the kids are in bed. There is no right or wrong time or place to pray. Consistency is the key.

As Richard J. Foster so eloquently puts it in *Prayer: Finding the Heart's True Home*: "To pray is to change. This is a great grace. How good of God to provide a path whereby our lives can be taken over by love and joy and peace and patience and kindness and goodness and faithfulness and gentleness and self-control."[54]

Reflection Exercise

Find your favorite spot. It may be in your living room or your bedroom or a daily route that you jog or walk. It may be in your car or in your bed, first thing in the morning or last thing at night.

When you are ready to pray, take a few deep breaths to relax your body. You may choose a Scripture or centering word to quiet your busy mind. It sometimes helps to have a notebook and pen in hand to write down distracting thoughts. Getting them out of your mind and onto paper often allows you to turn your attention to spiritual things.

Once you are quiet, listen to what rises up from within your spirit. This will lead you into a conversation with God. You may have questions to ask. Ask, expecting to receive an answer. Tell the Lord what is on your heart. Be honest with God. Bare your vulnerable places. And then, once you've emptied your heart, simply listen. God has much to say to you. You may want to write down what you hear, or you may simply want to receive.

Reflection Exercise

■ Where do you most often meet God? Nature? Bible study? Service? Worship? Journaling?

■ How might you establish a pattern of going there to pray on a consistent basis?

■ In what way do you most often pray? Do you feel "pot-bound"? Might God be calling you to a new prayer avenue?

■ What kind of prayer will help you more often to be aware of Jesus' presence within you?

18

Meditation

When we are not afraid to enter into our own center and to concentrate on the stirrings of our own soul, we come to know that being alive means being loved. This experience tells us that we can only love because we are born out of love, that we can only give because our life is a gift.
—Henri Nouwen, *The Wounded Healer: Ministry in Contemporary Society*[55]

Meditation saved my life.

I wrote the poem "Rivers of Living Water" during Joel's early adolescence after an amazing meditation that overflowed with light, love, and living water. While the poem speaks to a mountaintop experience (and for thirty minutes, I *was* on a mountaintop!), this was not a time of spiritual highs. These were desert years, when hormones were the match that lit the fuse of already out-of-whack brain chemicals. The entire family rode Joel's manic episodes like a roller coaster; agitation, aggression, and nonstop movement two weeks out of every six; up and down, up and down, up and down. There were many days I didn't know how much longer I could hang on for the ride.

> Rivers of Living Water
> John 7:38
>
> Within my center
> soul exists a chamber

beautiful beyond telling
where springs of living water flow
into stream, river, sea
of liquid love and pulsing light

Here I rock in Mother arms
rest in Father love
this sanctum my harbor
a mooring place
to let down sails of self
lover, mother, daughter, friend
tattered and
in need of mending

Naked I immerse myself
baptize my brokenness
break blue waters like a fish
dripping, trembling, alive
Alive!

Conduit of electric love
I unfurl sails
hoist up anchor
journey back to solid ground
on rivers of living water

Meditation was, and still is, my lifeline, my secret place to meet with God. Meditation brings order in the midst of chaos, peace in upheaval, certainty in times of uncertainty. Meditation brings me joy in the middle of sadness, cool, fresh water in times of drought. Most importantly, meditation brings me into the Lord's presence, and it is there that I know, deep down to my bones, that I am God's beloved.

Meditation

I began practicing the discipline of Christian meditation (also known as contemplative prayer) more than thirty years ago, shortly after my father's death. My dad and I were very close, and losing him shook my world to its core. His death was the seminal event that opened my eyes to God's very real presence in my life. I'd been raised in the church but was a prodigal daughter during my high school and college years. God used my dad's death to draw me back to Jesus.

As I learned the discipline of meditation, I began to take great delight in coming into the Lord's presence with no agenda and no requests—simply sitting and waiting for God.

THROUGHOUT the past thirty years, I have taught many people to meditate, both individually and in groups. I have also done healing prayer work with several cancer patients, helping them to visualize and meditate on the light of Christ moving throughout their bodies to eradicate cancer cells.

Many Christians are leery of meditation. The word itself conjures up images of men in white robes chanting while sitting lotus fashion. Christian meditation is not to be confused with Transcendental Meditation (TM), brought to the West from India. Here are a few points of contrast to note:

■ Eastern meditation puts a focus on emptying the mind, whereas Christian meditation teaches us to empty the mind in order to fill it with the presence of God.

■ Eastern meditation teaches its practitioners to detach from the world. Christian meditation helps us detach from the noise and chaos of the world in order to gain a richer attachment to God and to the people around us.

■ Eastern meditation advocates losing individuality in order to merge with the Cosmic Mind. Christian meditation stresses transformation into the wholeness for which God created us—becoming more like Christ. A regular discipline of meditation allows that transformation to take place as we spend time in God's presence.

In the silence, we come face-to-face with our own shortcomings and sinfulness. But we are also met by the grace of an ever-forgiving God in that silence. It's in this continuous meeting that we gradually let go of many of our unhealthy compulsions and the masks we've worn for so long to protect ourselves. We become, over time, more and more the person God created us to be. This transformation can't help but spill outward, making our lives and our ministries more effective, blessing those with whom we come into contact. Richard J. Foster writes that, for this reason, meditation is the most practical of all the spiritual disciplines.[56]

The Bible is full of references to meditation, as well as reasons to meditate:

> Happy are those . . .
> [whose] delight is in the law of the LORD,
> and on his law they meditate day and night.
> They are like trees planted by streams of water. (Psalm 1:1-3, NRSV)

> Be still before the LORD, and wait patiently for him. (Psalm 37:7, NRSV)

> For God alone my soul waits in silence;
> from him comes my salvation. (Psalm 62:1, NRSV)

> If the Spirit of him who raised Jesus from the dead dwells in you, he who raised Christ from the dead will give life to your mortal bodies also through his Spirit that dwells in you. (Romans 8:11, NRSV)

Meditation is paying attention to the presence of the Holy Spirit within us.

▪ In learning to meditate, we accept Jesus' invitation to overflowing life in him: "I came that they may have life, and have it abundantly" (John 10:10, NRSV).
▪ In meditation, we intentionally leave the distractions of the world and self behind, and come into the light of Christ. "I am the light of the world. Who-

ever follows me will never walk in darkness but will have the light of life" (John 8:12, NRSV). The life and light of Jesus are found within all who trust in him. ▨ When we meditate, we practice abiding in the vine that is Jesus. "I am the vine, you are the branches. Those who abide in me and I in them bear much fruit, because apart from me you can do nothing" (John 15:5, NRSV).

Great Christian thinkers and writers throughout the ages have written of the importance of and the joy that comes from the discipline of meditation, including the desert fathers of the fourth and fifth centuries, Augustine of Hippo, Francis of Assisi, Julian of Norwich, Brother Lawrence, George Fox, Evelyn Underhill, Thomas Merton, Thomas Kelly, Henri Nouwen, Richard J. Foster, Thomas Keating, and John Main.

Theophan, a Russian mystic, wrote, "To pray is to descend with the mind into the heart, and there to stand before the face of the Lord, ever-present, all seeing, within you."[57] Like Theophan, many of the saints throughout Christian history have written about using a centering word or Scripture as a tool to descend from the head to the heart. The quiet repetition of a single word or phrase helps us move from busy mind to centered heart. Some examples to add to those suggested previously include the Jesus Prayer ("Jesus Christ, Son of the living God, have mercy on me") and Psalm 23 ("The Lord is my shepherd, I shall not want").

Meditation is not magic. It is not "New Age." It is simply a tool that helps us to concentrate, to move to the center, to create an inner stillness so that we might listen for and hear the voice of God. When distracting thoughts come to mind, it helps to have a place to come back to. When you find your mind wandering, just gently bring it back to your Scripture or centering word. Let your thoughts roll by like pictures on a movie screen without judging them.

Walking meditation is more effective for those of us who have a hard time sitting still. To practice this meditation, choose a quiet place to walk, preferably a place where you can take in the beauty of God's creation. Don't rush. Walk at a temperate pace, repeating your centering word or

Scripture in rhythm with your footsteps. Let your eyes drink in God's presence in creation.

You can also meditate while lying on a blanket in the grass, gazing heavenward as clouds float by. Try it while walking the beach, watching the waves roll in. Try it while listening to contemplative music. I've found that, as with any type of prayer, consistency of time and space is important. It helps to establish a rhythm of prayer that you come to expect and look forward to within the structure of your day.

One of the priceless gifts of meditation is that we not only come to a deeper knowledge of God, but we come to realize how deeply we are known by God. Curt Thompson writes of this two-way process of "being known" in *Anatomy of the Soul*:

> The practice of meditation . . . puts us in position to be open to God's search of us. It enables us to be aware of our bodies and how God may be speaking to us through them. It does not simply help us focus on something else (God's law, precepts, or deeds) but facilitates the process by which we focus on Someone Else focusing on us. When we look deeply into someone else's eyes, we not only see the person's eyes, we see our being seen by them. This reflects the experience of being known.[58]

When we practice meditation, it slowly leads us to an experience of deep rest in God's active presence. After a time, we find ourselves taking this prayer with us into our daily lives. We can breathe this prayer when we're stuck in traffic or when anxiety begins to rise. Meditation is a very simple activity that, with time, becomes as natural as breathing. We don't need any special gifts to be able to meditate. We only need the burning desire to know—and be known by—God.

Reflection Exercise

Find a quiet place where you will not be disturbed. Choose a centering word or Scripture text.

- Sit comfortably, feet flat on the floor, shoes off if possible.
- Place your hands palms up on your lap.
- Take several deep breaths in and out, breathing from the belly.
- Notice any tension in your body. Wiggle the muscles of the places in your body where you feel tension.
- Begin to repeat your centering word or Scripture in your mind. Repeat it slowly, along with your breathing. (Repeat it in rhythm with your steps if you choose to walk instead of sit.)
- When thoughts come to mind (which they certainly will), simply let them float across your field of vision like pictures on a movie screen. Try not to hold on to them.
- If you find yourself only thinking thoughts instead of repeating your centering phrase or Scripture, do not judge yourself. Simply bring your mind back to your centering word or phrase.
- Give yourself grace. At first this will feel extremely foreign and contrived. It takes time and it takes practice. But in the end, it is well worth it as you descend into deep quiet where the still, small voice of God can be heard.

19

Lectio Divina

There is only one way of reading that is congruent with our Holy Scriptures. . . . This is the kind of reading named by our ancestors as *lectio divina*, often translated as "spiritual reading," reading that enters our souls as food, enters our stomachs, spreads through our blood, and becomes holiness and love and wisdom.
—Eugene H. Peterson, *Eat This Book: A Conversation in the Art of Spiritual Reading*[59]

In her book *Sacred Rhythms: Arranging Our Lives for Spiritual Transformation*, Ruth Haley Barton talks about the difference between reading the Scriptures for information and reading them for transformation.[60] Suddenly, as I read her words, I am transported to 1979, the year God drew me back to faith.

My father had just died, and God had revealed himself to me through a powerful dream. I wanted to get to know this God who loved me enough to comfort me in my grief. And so Wally and I began attending church with my mother. We hadn't been to church in years, other than Christmas and Easter services.

I accepted an invitation to join a women's Bible study. I don't remember what the study covered. I only remember that everyone in the group was given a study guide to read at home, a guide full of questions that seemed shallow and self-explanatory to me. Why was I being asked to write down what Jesus said? His words were right there, in the Bible! I remember feeling irritated with the process and very much an outsider in the group.

When the group gathered once a month, we went through the questions, one by one, taking turns speaking out loud what we'd written in our little guides. There were no questions about how the verses impacted our personal lives. There was no time set aside to meditate on the Scripture. The words we were reading and studying did not seem to have any relevance to my own life as a young mother. It all seemed so foreign and far away to me—these words written two thousand years ago. I felt as if something was wrong with me. I wanted to be a good Christian. Why weren't the Scriptures meaningful to me? Where was the personal God who reached through time and space to touch me at the deepest place of my grief over losing Dad?

It took me more than fifteen years to realize that I was starving for the ways in which the Word intersected with my life.

Fast-forward fifteen years. Meditation had become a lifeline for me as I navigated the waters of losing my dad, raising three boys, and parenting a son with autism. But meditation is a solitary activity, and I still felt like an outsider in traditional Bible studies. When invited to join a contemplative prayer group with three other women, I jumped at the chance. Our first time together I experienced an amazing sense of coming home, of belonging.

Cheryl, Jackie, Mary Sue, and I gathered every other week, sitting in silence, simply waiting for the still, small voice of God. In the quiet, we meditated, read our Bibles, or wrote in journals. After an hour of silence, we shared what we heard in the quiet. My hunger for the Spirit was satiated each time we met.

Our times together were so satisfying that we soon began meeting weekly. Jackie, who is an Episcopal priest, suggested one day that we try practicing *lectio divina*. I had no idea how hungry I'd been until we began this ancient practice of spiritual reading. It has been life-changing.

LECTIO *divina*, or "divine reading," is an ancient practice with roots in the desert fathers and early monasticism. The practice is experiencing a resurgence today as believers seek to connect with the Scriptures on a more personal level—to experience God's love more deeply through the Word. Rather than reading the Scriptures to gain information or insight into the historical context, it is a way of *abiding* with the Word of God.

In *lectio divina* we listen with the ears of our hearts. We listen for God's voice—the voice that Elijah heard on the mountain—the voice he heard not in the wind, not in the earthquake, not in the fire—but in a gentle whisper (1 Kings 19:11-13). In order to hear a whisper, we need to learn to be silent. The spiritual discipline of *lectio divina* helps us to do this.

After beginning in silence (*silencio*), *lectio divina* consists of four movements that can be practiced individually or within a small group: *lectio*, *meditatio*, *oratio*, and *contemplatio*. Practicing *lectio divina* in a group is powerful. It has been so transformational in my own life over the past twelve years with my contemplative prayer group that I now lead two additional groups. The instructions below are written for a group format. If practicing on your own, simply write your answers in a journal rather than sharing them out loud.

Silencio (silence). Begin by sitting in silence or with meditative music to prepare your hearts to meet God in the Scripture. This is a time of expectancy, knowing that when you open yourselves to the presence of the Holy Spirit, you receive the gift of God's presence, which is with us always.

Lectio (read). One person in the group reads a short portion of Scripture aloud slowly. It is important not to rush the reading. Listen for one word or phrase that grabs your attention—that shimmers—that speaks to you in a way you can't ignore. You may experience an unpleasant visceral reaction, or you may be overcome with a feeling of peace. Pay attention to your body *and* mind as the Word is read aloud. Each person in the circle shares the word that speaks to them with the rest of the group without adding any explanation.

Meditatio (meditation). Another person reads the Scripture aloud slowly again, perhaps from a different translation. If you are the reader, roll the words around in your mind and heart. Listen again for one word or phrase that shimmers with energy. It may be a different word or phrase from the first reading. Then sit with the word, asking God where it intersects with your life situation today. This is not a time to figure out what God is saying to the world or what the overall theology of the word is. This is a time to ask, "What are you saying to *me*, Lord, today, through this word? What part of my daily life does this speak to?" Sit in silence and ponder this in your heart for a few minutes. When you feel ready, share with the group as much as you're comfortable sharing. Depending on the size of your group, this time of sharing may take fifteen to thirty minutes.

Oratio (respond). Still another person reads the Scripture aloud slowly and meditatively, and then the group enters once more into the quiet. Again, you are listening for one particular word or phrase that carries energy with it. This time, listen as well for God's invitation. As you look at the way this word intersects with your life, ask God what the Spirit is inviting you to—is there some action, some challenge, or some change that God is suggesting? It is good to set aside at least thirty minutes of silence after this reading. If it is a nice day, your group might find places to sit outside, alone, for this extended time of silence.

Contemplatio (contemplation). Finally, after you have responded to God's invitation in your hearts, simply rest in God's presence, soaking up God's love. At the end of this movement, gather again to share what God has written on your hearts during the silence.

This method of reading the Scriptures is transformational: "For the word of God is alive and active. Sharper than any double-edged sword, it penetrates even to dividing soul and spirit, joints and marrow; it judges the thoughts and attitudes of the heart" (Hebrews 4:12, NIV).

In the three groups that practice *lectio divina* of which I am a part, I have watched, week after week, as God works on a deep level to shape and transform lives, mine included. Below is one of my journal entries from a time of *lectio* when I was struggling with helping Joel make the transition from our home to his new home at Safe Haven Farms:

> Today's Scripture text is Philippians 3:7-16. The verse that catches my attention, on all three read-throughs, is verse 12b: "Christ Jesus has made me his own."

As I sit in the silence with this verse, repeating it over and over as a centering word, a recent dream rises to mind.

In the dream, I approach a wounded bird. It is a sandhill crane with a huge wingspan. The bird is on the ground, and someone else (my husband?) is attempting to care for it. I want to tend to this beautiful, wounded bird, so I continue my approach, my hand held out in a gesture of peace. The terrified bird flails around, its great wings beating a tattoo on the ground. I am afraid she will be hurt in her frightened fury. I stop and whisper, "Shhh. It's okay. I'm here to help. Stop struggling. I'm here."

The crane eventually abandons her struggle, and I stroke her graceful, feathered neck.

As I sit in the silence with this dream, I wonder if I am the wounded bird or the person tending her. As the mother of a son with autism, my wounds are deep. Many of these wounds have healed over the years as I've come to a place where I can accept my son just as he is. But some of the wounds have reopened in the past eighteen months since we moved Joel to Safe Haven Farms. I find myself unable to surrender him to God for safekeeping. My mind spins constantly with worries and fears and concerns for his safety, happiness, and overall well-being. After all, who can care for my son as well as his father and I?

Yes, I believe I am the wounded bird, flailing and thrashing, afraid to let even God close enough to tend to my wounds.

But am I also the one tending the bird? My son is wounded. This move has been difficult for him, and I am trying so hard to comfort him. To let him know he will be okay. That I am still here. I will always be his mother. I will never abandon him.

I get up from my prayer chair to Google "crane," to see what this dream symbol might mean. Birds themselves symbolize our goals, aspirations, and hopes. Cranes, in particular, symbolize happiness, maternal love, and gestures of goodwill. They are a symbol of looking out for those you love. Cranes can also symbolize a person's strength, uniqueness, or individuality, and also persistence through challenges. They may be telling you that you have too much of one of these qualities or could benefit by being less this way.

I go back into the quiet, asking God to reveal what he is saying to me through this dream. This is what I hear with the ears of my heart:

Yes, Kathy, you are the injured crane, flailing around with worry and anxiety about your son. You have been so strong all these years—always the caregiver—you have persisted through many challenges. But now is the time to stop struggling. Simply "be" in my presence. I am here. You're okay. Lean into my presence. Again I say, stop struggling. You will injure those beautiful wings. Those wings represent your aspirations, hopes, and dreams for the future. You were meant to fly. This is the way to learn how to fly. Spend more time in the Word and in my presence. Be with me, Kathy. Stop struggling.

Here is the invitation I am hearing today: God is saying to me, *I have made you my own. I gave you those wings. It's time to let go. It's time to fly.*

Reflection Exercise

Set aside an hour to explore the spiritual discipline of *lectio divina*, following the steps of the group experience described above. If you're so led, ask a friend, a small group, or your spouse to accompany you on this adventure. Choose a familiar Scripture or make a choice from the lectionary. (I use the Revised Common Lectionary at http://lectionary.library.vanderbilt.edu.) As a group or on your own, follow the movements explained above.

At the end of the extended silence, regather as a group and share what bubbled up in the quiet, focusing on God's personal invitation to you. Share only as much as you are comfortable sharing. Close your time together with a prayer.

20

Worship

A disciple once came to Abba Joseph, saying, "Father, according as I am able, I keep my little rule, my little fast, and my little prayer. And according as I am able, I strive to cleanse my mind of all evil thoughts and my heart of all evil intents. Now, what more should I do?" Abba Joseph rose up and stretched out his hands to heaven, and his fingers became like ten lamps of fire. He answered, "Why not be totally changed into fire?"
—Richard J. Foster, *Prayer: Finding the Heart's True Home*[61]

Yesterday in church, my son Joel stood beside me as tall and straight as a young poplar tree. That may not sound remarkable to you. But my son never stands straight and tall. As well as autism, Joel has severe kyphosis of the spine. While scoliosis manifests as an S curve, kyphosis appears as a C curve, or hunchback.

And yet yesterday Joel stood a good two or three inches taller than usual. An inner fire lit up his face, the smile lines around his eyes crinkled endearingly, and he managed some fancy dance moves despite the fact that we were crowded into tight rows of chairs.

Once again I entered the school of worship with Joel as my teacher.

In writing and speaking about ways to make our churches more inclusive for people with disabilities, I often refer to the importance of using a multisensory approach. Children with special needs benefit from Sunday school lessons and worship that use all five senses: kinesthetic, auditory, visual, olfactory, and gustatory. (Information on Margot Hausmann's wonderful resource sheet, "Multisensory Worship Ideas," which tells how to use the senses in a worship setting, is found in "Further Resources" at the end of this book.)

Joel has been teaching me about worship for more than twenty-five years (see my earlier books, *His Name Is Joel: Searching for God in a Son's Disability, A Place Called Acceptance: Ministry with Families of Children with Disabilities,* and *Autism & Alleluias,* for examples), and evidently he isn't done teaching me yet. Yesterday he took me to a whole new level of understanding what Adele Ahlberg Calhoun meant when she wrote in *Spiritual Disciplines Handbook,* "The heart of worship is to seek to know and love God in our own unique way."[62]

Yesterday I watched Joel worship with abandon. He did not waste one bit of energy on what the people surrounding him thought. He simply gave God his all. I couldn't help but think of Jesus' response to the young man who asked him, "'Teacher, which is the greatest commandment in the Law?' Jesus responded, "'Love the Lord your God with all your heart and with all your soul and with all your mind.' This is the first and greatest commandment" (Matthew 22:36-38, NIV).

I have to ask myself, how often do I do that?

How often do you do that?

THE BIBLICAL accounts of avenues of worship are many. Yesterday John, the pastor of our little Vineyard Church, broke it down into several categories. Joel listened carefully to each one and responded—body, mind, and spirit—to them all. (This is a young man who has a difficult time sitting still and attending for more than five minutes at a time.)

▪ *Shouting.* The Psalms, especially, are full of references to shouting in worship: "Shout for joy to the LORD, all the earth, burst into jubilant song with music" (Psalm 98:4, NIV). "Shout for joy to the LORD, all the earth. Worship the LORD with gladness; come before him with joyful songs" (Psalm 100:1-2, NIV). Joel's eyes grew wide as John demonstrated, shouting praises to God.

Joel's quizzical expression seemed to ask, "Shouting, in church? Really?" And then a big grin answered his unspoken question: "Sounds good to me!"

■ *Proclamation.* We worship when we declare what God has done for us, remember where he has met us, and proclaim the holiness and greatness of God: "Sing the praises of the LORD, enthroned in Zion; proclaim among the nations what he has done" (Psalm 9:11, NIV). "I will proclaim the name of the LORD. Oh, praise the greatness of our God!" (Deuteronomy 32:3, NIV). After the message, as we went into worship, John had us shout out our own proclamations of God's goodness. I looked at Joel and proclaimed, "God, you are so good to me!" Joel followed suit, his grin widening by the moment as he whispered, "I love Jesus!"

■ *Reading the Word.* Power and life flows from the Word of God as it is read aloud: "They stood where they were and read from the Book of the Law of the LORD their God for a quarter of the day, and spent another quarter in confession and in worshiping the LORD their God" (Nehemiah 9:3, NIV). "As the rain and the snow come down from heaven, and do not return to it without watering the earth and making it bud and flourish, so that it yields seed for the sower and bread for the eater, so is my word that goes out from my mouth: It will not return to me empty, but will accomplish what I desire and achieve the purpose for which I sent it" (Isaiah 55:10-11, NIV). Joel sat forward in his seat, listening intently as John read several Scriptures to the congregation.

■ *Singing and playing an instrument.* The Bible is full of references to worshipping the Lord with instruments: "David and all the Israelites were celebrating with all their might before God, with songs and with harps, lyres, timbrels, cymbals and trumpets" (1 Chronicles 13:8, NIV). "Praise him with trumpet sound; praise him with lute and harp! Praise him with tambourine and dance; praise him with strings and pipe!" (Psalm 150:3-4, NRSV). Joel played an air guitar in response to John's listing of several instruments that we can use to worship the Lord.

■ *Clapping.* We can praise God with our bodies, including our hands: "Clap your hands, all you nations; shout to God with cries of joy" (Psalm 47:1, NIV).

This time Joel didn't wait for John to demonstrate. He clapped his hands with enthusiasm, drawing the entire congregation into noisy worship. Joel wasn't the only person grinning at this point in the service!

▪ *Being still.* We worship God as we wait for the Lord in the quiet: "For God alone my soul waits in silence; from him comes my salvation" (Psalm 62:1, NRSV). "Be still before the LORD, and wait patiently for him" (Psalm 37:7, NIV). Again, Joel sat upright in his chair, eyes on Pastor John, listening closely to the Scripture.

▪ *Lifting hands to the Lord.* "Lift up your hands in the sanctuary and praise the LORD" (Psalm 134:2, NIV). These outward forms of worship require us to remove stumbling blocks of self-consciousness or pride that stand in our way of abandoning ourselves to something that might be out of the ordinary in some church settings. As John demonstrated, Joel joined him by standing up and lifting his hands in a "touch down" pose, cheering on the Holy Spirit team.

▪ *Dancing.* When we're "all in" for God, we may be able to let down our defenses and dance before the Lord: "David danced before the LORD with all his might; David was girded with a linen ephod. So David and all the house of Israel brought up the ark of the LORD with shouting, and with the sound of the trumpet" (2 Samuel 6:14-15, NRSV). Joel began shuffling his feet. He lifted them up, one by one, and stomped on the ground. The woman sitting in front of us turned to see what was making the floor shake. A smile replaced her frown as she saw Joel dancing from his chair. When we went into worship after the sermon, Joel took his dance moves to a whole new level.

▪ *Singing a new song.* When our hearts are open to God and the movement of the Spirit, our very lives can become a new song: "Praise the LORD with the lyre, make melody to him with the harp of ten strings. Sing to him a new song; play skillfully on the strings, with loud shouts" (Psalm 33:2-3, NRSV). John encouraged the congregation to sing new songs as we go about our days, making up uncomplicated tunes and putting them to the simplest of lyrics: "I love you, Lord. You are my Rock. You are my Redeemer. Thank you, Lord. Thank you." Again, during worship we were given a few moments to make up our own new songs. The room hummed with a beautiful cacophony of songs. Joel joined in with a simple "I love my God." Radiance poured from his face as he looked around the worship space, soaking in the abandonment of structure as new, individual, and unique songs emerged. For someone with autism, this was a huge learning curve, a new level of healing.

■ *Bowing down.* Kneeling before the Lord is an act of submission and humility: "O come, let us worship and bow down, let us kneel before the LORD, our Maker! For he is our God, and we are the people of his pasture, and the sheep of his hand" (Psalm 95:6, NRSV).

I have never, in the more than twenty-five years that we've been bringing Joel to church, seen him tune in to a sermon like he did this one. After the sermon was over and we entered into worship as a congregation, it was as if a dam had burst. Joel worshipped God with heart, soul, strength, and mind. He danced, hands held over his head, singing the words he knew and smiling through the ones he didn't know. He clapped, he stomped his feet, he sang his heart out.

When was the last time I worshipped with absolute abandon?

When was the last time you worshipped in this manner?

Jessica Leah Springer writes, "As John 4:23 says, it's time, as worshipers of God, to give him all we have. For when he is exalted, everything about me is decreased. So many times we stand in the way of really stepping into the secret place of worship with God. Just abandon tradition and the 'expected' ways of Praise & Worship and get lost in the holy of holies with the sole intention of blessing the Father's heart."[63]

For Joel, abandoning tradition is an easy thing to do. He's not bound by rules and expectations of what others think. He doesn't wear a mask to protect himself from others' critiques. He is simply himself, and because of that, he comes before God as he is, not as he wishes to be known.

In the words of N. T. Wright, "We meet with the high and holy one, the God of fire, in order that we may ourselves be transformed and be agents for the healing of this world. . . . To enjoy worship for its own sake, or simply out of a cultural appreciation of the 'performance,' would be like Moses coming upon a burning bush and deciding to cook his lunch on it."[64]

Looking back, I realize I was standing on holy ground as I worshipped with Joel yesterday. I should have taken off my shoes. My son stood so close to the burning bush that he, himself, caught on fire. I watched him transform from a slumped-over young man with developmental disabilities and autism into the tall, confident, joyful young man we don't often see with our earthly eyes. Because of the sparks that were thrown off from his being, I also met with the High and Holy One, the God of fire.

May each of us, through our abandonment in worship, become agents of transformation and healing for this broken world in which we live.

Reflection Exercise

Dare yourself to try a new avenue of worship this week—shouting, clapping, bowing down, dancing, silence—some form of worship you don't normally engage in. You can do this in the privacy of your home, while you're out for a walk, or if you're feeling adventurous, in church. Notice your bodily sensations as you worship in a new manner. Notice your feelings. You may want to journal your experience.

For Further Reflection
■ Read Psalm 150.
■ Consider how you worship the Lord. In what ways does your praise manifest? When was the last time you worshipped with abandon?
■ You may think of worship as one-way communication with God—you communicating your love for God. C. S. Lewis writes in *Reflections on the Psalms*, "It is in the process of being worshipped that God communicates His presence to men."[65]
■ This week, as you worship at home and at church, pay attention to what God is communicating to you.

21

Celebration

Applause, everyone. Bravo, bravissimo! Shout God-songs at the top of
your lungs!
—Psalm 47:1, MSG

Joel loves to dance. He's a study in joy on the dance floor—arms flailing, feet
shuffling, eyes shining. Joy bubbles up in my veins as I watch him, inviting me
to get up and do my own celebratory dance.

I find myself asking, "When was the last time I celebrated? Truly celebrated?"

Celebration brings joy, and joy makes us strong. The prophet Nehemiah reminds us that the joy of the LORD is our strength (Nehemiah 8:10). Richard J.
Foster writes in his classic *Celebration of Discipline*, "Celebration is central to
all the Spiritual Disciplines. Without a joyful spirit of festivity the Disciplines become dull, death-breathing tools in the hands of modern Pharisees. Every Discipline should be characterized by carefree gaiety and a sense of thanksgiving."[66]

How do we celebrate? Watch Joel at a dance or watch any five-year-old at a
birthday party, and you will find the answer. We celebrate with singing, dancing,
shouts of joy, and laughter as we unleash our creativity and use our imagination.
But these seem to be spontaneous expressions of joy. Where is the discipline
involved? Is celebration something that requires conscious cultivation?

Our culture celebrates rites of passage, such as birthdays, weddings, graduations, and anniversaries. We celebrate with music, food, drink, and sometimes pageantry. As for our daily lives, many of us go about with our heads
down, grinding through mountains of e-mails, running from meeting to meet-

ing or from one doctor's appointment to the next, checking off our to-do lists as we go. Celebrating in the midst of the humdrum of our days can seem a bit foreign.

Paul gave the church in Philippi some hints on cultivating a sense of joy and celebration: "Rejoice in the Lord always. I will say it again: Rejoice! Let your gentleness be evident to all. The Lord is near. Do not be anxious about anything, but in every situation, by prayer and petition, with thanksgiving, present your requests to God. And the peace of God, which transcends all understanding, will guard your hearts and your minds in Christ Jesus" (Philippians 4:4-7, NIV). In good times and hard times, rejoice. Lay all anxieties at the foot of the cross—by prayer, *with thanksgiving*. We're not asked to thank God for the suffering of disability or disease, but to thank God that the Lord is near to us in the midst of the hard times.

Paul goes on to write, "Finally, brothers and sisters, whatever is true, whatever is noble, whatever is right, whatever is pure, whatever is lovely, whatever is admirable—if anything is excellent or praiseworthy—think about such things" (Philippians 4:8, NIV).

In other words, celebration is a frame of mind, a set of lenses through which we view the world. Keeping our minds focused on the positive when our minds are prone to get hung up on the negative requires an act of the will. With discipline, by choosing where we allow our thoughts to settle, we can actually change the way our brains are wired: "Do not conform to the pattern of this world, but be transformed be the renewing of your mind" (Romans 12:2, NIV). Like learning to play the piano or learning to meditate, cultivating the discipline of celebration in daily life requires conscious effort and practice. (For an exciting and extensive explanation of how the brain is wired and how we can change that wiring through the spiritual disciplines, among other exercises, read *Anatomy of the Soul* by Curt Thompson, MD.[67])

MY FRIEND Annette makes celebration an art form. Annette also knows suffering and disability. She was severely injured in a car accident as a young woman and spent months in bed recovering. She was diagnosed with crippling rheumatoid arthritis in her thirties. Annette was healed of arthritis during a healing service at a local church. It was not an instantaneous healing, but over months and years of soaking prayer, Annette found total healing, a healing she attributes to the power of the blood of Jesus. She has devoted her life, over the past twenty-five years, to spreading news of the healing power of Jesus throughout the world through her ministry, Bridge for Peace.

To spend a day in Annette's presence is to spend a day in celebration. We only see each other twice a year, and when we're together we go out for coffee and conversation. Sharing a latte with Annette is like winning the lottery. We celebrate by singing, dancing, laughing, sharing stories, and just plain having fun.

As for big celebrations? No one does it better. Annette arranges Praise Cruises and Praise Trolleys—days of exuberant worship and praise filled with laughter and fun—for her ministry. She created the Festival of Kings, a celebration every Epiphany, during which ministry members dress up in costumes representing the magi. My husband and I have known about the festival for years but had never been able to travel to New York to participate until this year. Playing dress-up—fashioning crowns out of wrapping paper and glue—we laughed until tears streaked our faces, giddy as kids who've eaten too much sugar. After an hour of laughter and picture-taking in our outlandish outfits, we solemnly processed up a hill and into the mission house, and worshipped until we were led to place our crowns, one by one, at the foot of the manger set up in the living room. It was an awesome evening that combined creativity, imagination, laughter, shouts of joy, singing, praise, and worship.

That's celebration.

A celebration of a different sort—more of the daily variety—took place this past weekend. Wally and I were scheduled to help out at the monthly dance held at Joel's home, Safe Haven Farms. We look forward to these dances. Just watching my son dance is a guarantee of entering into a little piece of heaven on earth. But this particular night, for whatever reason, Joel was agitated and anxious, unable to relax. He walked into the brightly decorated multipurpose room where music was blaring, took one look around, and turned on his heel, running for the door. Dan, his one-on-one staff, followed closely behind.

Within five minutes, Joel returned. He refused to sit down for dinner, which had just been served. Out the door he ran again. I continued dishing up food, watching my son run in and out of the building several times over the course of twenty minutes. Finally, Wally whispered in my ear, "Let's go."

Parents know when agitation teeters on the edge of a full-blown meltdown. It was definitely time for a fast exit. We apologized to the other parent volunteers for leaving them in the lurch, gathered up Joel's backpack and meds, shepherded him to the car, and headed toward our home, where he was scheduled to spend the night.

Just seven o'clock on a beautiful evening, bedtime was still a couple of hours away. We decided to take a cruise on our new pontoon boat, located just up the road from our house. A visual mantle of relaxation settled over Joel the moment he stepped onto the boat. Touring around the lake at a leisurely pace, we surprised at least ten great blue herons from their rookery in a tree near the bank. We watched in awe as they took off in flight, lifting into the air with great, measured strokes.

We sang Joel's favorite praise songs—"This Is the Day," "I Love You, Lord," and "This Little Light of Mine." After singing, Joel hunkered down in a lawn chair on the front of the boat, peering out from under the bill of his baseball cap, relishing the wind in his face. I felt my body and spirit release all tension as his eyes crinkled up with a face-transforming smile. "Thank you, God," I whispered.

Toward the end of the ride, a flash of silver to the right of the boat caught my eye. I turned to see a bald eagle flying past with a fish in his beak. Wally turned off the boat's engine, and we sat for several minutes, watching with rapt attention as this majestic bird landed in the top of a tree and devoured his catch, white head bobbing up and down as he tore at his prey.

This evening we *celebrated*. It wasn't a special occasion. As a matter of fact, we'd narrowly avoided what could have been a major meltdown. It was a perfectly ordinary Saturday evening in the middle of May. The lake reflected receding storm clouds, water and clouds alike fading to lavender in the slanting rays of the lowering sun. Herons continued winging over our heads with effortless beats of their great, wide wings. A beautiful wake streamed out behind the boat—waves that made Joel particularly happy because Joel has always had a love affair with waves. The three of us praised God, thankful for creation and for this time with one another.

> The world is filled with reasons to be downcast. But deeper than sorrow thrums the unbroken pulse of God's joy, a joy that will yet have its eternal day. To set our heart on this joy reminds us that we can choose how we respond to any particular moment. We can search for God in all circumstances, or not. We can seek the pulse of hope and celebration because it is God's reality. . . . Every small experience of Jesus with us is a taste of the joy that is to come. We are not alone—and that in itself is reason to celebrate.[68]

Reflection Exercise

Read Zephaniah 3:17 (ESV):

> The LORD your God is in your midst,
> a mighty one who will save;
> he will rejoice over you with gladness;
> he will quiet you by his love;
> he will exult over you with loud singing.

Close your eyes and take a few deep breaths. Tense and relax any muscles in your body that are holding on to tension. How do you imagine God rejoicing over you with gladness? Can you envision God quieting you with love? Exulting over you with loud singing? What feelings does this evoke within you? Take a few moments to journal your experience.

For Further Reflection

■ Consider Richard J. Foster's statement that celebration is central to all of the spiritual disciplines—that without it, the other disciplines are "dull, death-breathing tools in the hands of modern Pharisees." In what ways have you found this to be true in your own life? In what new ways might you celebrate the extraordinary in the midst of the ordinary? How might God be calling you to expand your capacity for joy in your everyday life?

■ How does your family celebrate rites of passage (birthdays, graduations, etc.)? Is there a way to weave your love of God into the celebration?

■ Bring to mind someone you know and respect who celebrates life's simple rhythms. In your mind's eye, watch the way he or she responds to the dailiness of life. What might you learn from this person? In what ways might you celebrate God's presence in the midst of the ordinary? How might God be calling you to expand your capacity for joy in your everyday life?

Afterword

Being a parent is a spiritual journey, period. Not many roles in our lives call up all the parts of who we are, heart, mind, body, and spirit, as does parenting, with all the joy, sweat, occasional (or frequent) heartbreak, and tears, that accompany our deep sense of call, commitment, and accomplishment. Spirituality is about our experiences of the sacred and holy. It is about faith, hope, and love. It is about our deepest beliefs and values, the ways we find and are given meaning in our lives. It is about connection, to self, to child, to spouse, to family, to others, to place and time, and to God, however defined.

The hundreds of parents of children with disabilities I have met and known over the past 40 years have been some of the most spiritual people I know. I think that comes because their spirit has to be addressed, grown, and nurtured to deal with the initial and ongoing realization that (1) life is not what we had planned and (2) we need amazing fluidity and resiliency of spirit to survive the ongoing cycles of love and loss, gratitude and frustration while searching for diagnoses, services, plans, programs, and mountains of red tape.

As in any physical discipline, the spirit only gains fluidity and resiliency through regular exercise—through movement. Such movement of the spirit comes through relationship, music, dance, painting, architecture, nature and more, things that we say capture our spirits and feelings or help them renew and even soar. No wonder, then, that we are seeing more and more art emanating from the lives of people with disabilities and their families.

Such artistry is the power of this book. Kathy Bolduc, mother of Joel, a young man on the autism spectrum approaching the old age of 30, is not writing a guidebook for parents of children with disabilities or special needs. Certainly she is writing out of her own Christian faith and tradition, but this is not a book that takes her journey and prescribes its maps and mileposts to others. Kathy has made the time and space to reflect on her journey through her writing in ways that enable her to find hope and meaning. She offers her experience, and the experiences of others, as creative experiments in the spiritual disciplines that fortify the whole person who is also parent of a child with disabilities.

The beauty of the book is that Kathy uses the languages of the soul and spirit: personal stories, encounters with other parents and their stories, quotations that become guideposts, Scriptures that have been sacred to her, symbols and suggestions. Hence the book's title, which describes the "spiritual art" of raising a child—and also her primary metaphor of the mosaic, beauty that emerges from the thousands of fragmented daily experiences and feelings. She is inviting and asking the readers to collect those fragments, to bring their own stories and make space to think about their own journey in ways that might help them find their own sacred moments, holy symbols, and passages that capture experience and meaning.

Kathy addresses themes of grief and brokenness, healing and self-care, meaningful ritual and routine, fellowship and community—themes that every parent will encounter and negotiate to find their own art form, for raising their child and children. She shares examples of how she has used ancient spiritual disciplines of prayer, meditation, *lectio divina*, worship, and celebration to discover ways that she is encountering both God's presence and absence in parts of her journey.

The purpose of this book is to focus attention on the help that comes from the Source beyond one's self. Parents of children with disabilities at any stage of their journey will be able to recognize in these pages parts of themselves, and perhaps perceive new mosaics in the blessings and broken pieces of their own lives. If you will, accept Kathy's offer and find your own rhythm, art form, or song. She will respect wherever you are and wherever you end up. Her focus is fixed, but her embrace is wide, with space for you to find your own creative movements in spirit and Spirit.

—Rev. Bill Gaventa
Director of Community and Congregational Supports

—Elizabeth M. Boggs Center on Developmental Disabilities
Executive Secretary, Religion and Spirituality Division
American Association on Intellectual and Developmental Disabilities

Notes

1. Morton T. Kelsey, *The Other Side of Silence: A Guide to Christian Meditation* (New York: Paulist, 1976), 27.
2. Merilee Tutcik, http://www.etsy.com/uk/people/Mtutcik, accessed September 30, 2013.
3. Quoted by Cai Emmons, http://theentangledwriter.blogspot.com /2010/11/broken-world.html, accessed September 30, 2013.
4. Cathy Cummings Chisholm, *Landscapes of the Heart* (Louisville: Bridge Resources, 1998), 9.
5. Eugene O'Neill, quoted in Anne Lamott, *Traveling Mercies: Some Thoughts on Faith* (New York: Random House, 1999), 112.
6. Kahlil Gibran, "On Joy and Sorrow," *The Prophet* (New York: Knopf, 1994), 29.
7. Wendell Berry, quoted in Anne Lamott, *Plan B: Further Thoughts on Faith* (New York: Riverhead, 2005), 39.
8. Anne Lamott, *Plan B*, 73.
9. Barbara Crooker, "Climbing the Jade Mountain," *Line Dance* (Cincinnati: Word Press, 2008). Used by permission.
10. Elisabeth Kübler-Ross, *On Death and Dying* (New York: Scribner, 1997).
11. Jacques Philippe, *Interior Freedom* (New York: Scepter, 2007), 134.
12. Carrie's baby was, indeed, born with myotonic dystrophy.
13. Parker Palmer, *A Hidden Wholeness: The Journey toward an Undivided Life* (San Francisco: Jossey-Bass, 2004), 5.
14. "Terry Tempest Williams: Finding Beauty in a Broken World," interview by David Medaris, *Isthmus, The Daily Page*, http://www.thedailypage.com/daily/article.php?article=24345.

15. Allen Ross, The Beatitudes, https://bible.org/seriespage/ beatitudes-matthew-51-12, accessed September 30, 2013.

16. Leonard Cohen, "Anthem," *Stranger Music* (Toronto: McClelland and Stewart, 1993). Used by permission.

17. Mother Teresa and Brian Kolodiejchuk, *Mother Teresa: Come Be My Light: The Private Writings of the Saint of Calcutta* (New York: Random House, 1997).

18. Thom M. Shuman, Pirate Jesus: Poems and Prayers for RCL Lectionary Year C (CreateSpace, Amazon.com, 2012).

19. Henri Nouwen, *Bread for the Journey: A Day Book of Wisdom and Faith* (New York, Harper Collins, 1997), 205.

20. Daniel Iverson, "Spirit of the Living God" (1926). Copyright © 1935, 1963 Birdwing Music (ASCAP). All rights reserved. Used by permission.

21. Macrina Wiederkehr, OSB, *Seasons of Your Heart: Prayers & Reflections* (San Francisco: HarperSanFrancisco, 1991). Used by permission.

22. M. Robert Mulholland Jr., *Invitation to a Journey: A Road Map for Spiritual Formation* (Downers Grove, IL: InterVarsity, 1993), 168.

23. William Shakespeare, *Macbeth* (II.ii.34).

24. Ann Voskamp, *One Thousand Gifts: A Dare to Live Fully Right Where You Are* (Grand Rapids: Zondervan, 2010), 172.

25. Barbara Crooker, "Simile," *Line Dance* (Cincinnati: Word Press, 2008). Used by permission.

26. Jon Kabat-Zinn, http://www.princeton.edu/uhs/pdfs/ Mindfulness-Lunch-Series.pdf (accessed September 27, 2013).

27. Barbara Crooker, "The Mother of a Handicapped Child Dreams of Respite," *Ordinary Life* (Edmund, OK: ByLine Press, 2001). Used by permission.

28. Barbara Crooker, "Autism Poem: The Grid," *Radiance* (Cincinnati: Word Press, 2005). Used by permission.

29. Adele Ahlberg Calhoun, *Spiritual Disciplines Handbook: Practices that Transform Us* (Downers Grove, IL: InterVarsity, 2005), 71.

30. Stephanie Paulsell, quoted in Ruth Haley Barton, *Sacred Rhythms: Arranging Our Lives for Spiritual Transformation* (Downers Grove, IL: InterVarsity, 2006), 78.

31. Calhoun, 72.

32. Howard Thurman, The Howard Thurman Center for Common Ground, www.bu.edu/thurman.

33. Madeleine L'Engle, *The Irrational Season: The Crosswicks Journal*, Book 3 (New York: HarperCollins, 1977), 47.

34. Curt Thompson, *Anatomy of the Soul: Surprising Connections between Neuroscience and Spiritual Practices That Can Transform Your Life and Relationships* (Carol Stream, IL: Tyndale, 2010), xiv.

35. Scott Hamilton, http://www.clevelandclinic.org/cancer/scottcares/scott/about.asp, accessed September 30, 2013.

36. Jean Vanier, quoted in Bill Clarke, S.J., *Enough Room for Joy: Jean Vanier's L'Arche, a Message for Our Time* (New York: Paulist, 1974), 141.

37. Henri Nouwen, *Bread for the Journey: A Day Book of Wisdom and Faith* (New York: HarperCollins, 1997), May 3, 2013. Henri Nouwen Society Daily Meditations, http://wp.henrinouwen.org/daily_meditation_blog/?p=2101, accessed September 30, 2013.

38. Ginny Thornburgh, ed., *That All May Worship: An Interfaith Welcome to People with Disabilities* (Washington, DC: National Organization on Disability, 1994), 4.

39. Ginny Thornburg, "Foreword," *Amazing Gifts: Stories of Faith, Disability, and Inclusion*, by Mark I. Pinsky (Herndon, VA: The Alban Institute, 2011).

40. Ibid.

41. Adele Ahlberg Calhoun, *Spiritual Disciplines Handbook: Practices That Transform Us* (Downers Grove, IL: InterVarsity, 2005), 121.

42. Henri Nouwen, *The Road to Daybreak: A Spiritual Journey* (New York: Doubleday, 1988), quoted on Goodreads, www.goodreads.com/quotes.

43. Henry T. Blackaby, Richard Blackaby, Claude V. King, *Experiencing God: Knowing and Doing the Will of God* (Nashville: B&H, 2008).

44. Henri Nouwen, *Life of the Beloved: Spiritual Living in a Secular World* (New York: Crossroads, 2002), 77–78.

45. Larry Kreider, *Authentic Spiritual Mentoring* (Ventura, CA: Regal, 2008).

46. Jolene Philo, *Different Dream Parenting: A Practical Guide to Raising a Child with Special Needs* (Grand Rapids: Discovery House, 2011).

47. Rick Warren, *The Purpose Driven Life: What on Earth Am I Here For?* (Grand Rapids: Zondervan, 2002).

48. Jean Vanier, *Community and Growth* (Mahwah, NJ: Paulist, 1989), quoted on Goodreads, www.goodreads.com/quotes.

49. Used with permission from Indiana Resource Center for Autism, www.iidc.indiana.edu/.index.php?pageId=32/, accessed October 12, 2013.

50. Quoted in Garnett E. Foster, "Spirituality for Leadership: History, Conflict and Challenge," 8. http://www.theoric.org /trinityfrench/benoitmazunda /Readings/Gen%20Readings /CC89BD1Bd01.pdf, accessed September 30, 2013.

51. Richard J. Foster, *Celebration of Discipline: The Path to Spiritual Growth* (San Francisco: Harper and Row, 1978), 30.

52. Richard J. Foster, *Prayer: Finding the Heart's True Home* (San Francisco: Harper and Row, 1992), 5.

53. Ruth Haley Barton, *Sacred Rhythms: Arranging Our Lives*

for Spiritual Transformation (Downers Grove, IL: InterVarsity, 2006), 63.

54. Foster, *Prayer*, 5.

55. Henri Nouwen, *The Wounded Healer: Ministry in Contemporary Society* (New York: Doubleday, 1979), 91.

56. Foster, *Celebration of* Discipline, 15.

57. Theophan, quoted by Henri Nouwen in *The Way of the Heart: The Spirituality of the Desert Fathers and Mothers* (New York: HarperCollins, 1981), 76.

58. Thompson, 176.

59. Eugene H. Peterson, *Eat This Book: A Conversation in the Art of Spiritual Reading* (Grand Rapids: Eerdmans, 2006), 4.

60. Barton, *Sacred Rhythms*.

61. Foster, *Prayer*, 6.

62. Calhoun, 45.

63. Jessica Leah Springer, http://chrisbowater.com/articles/quotes-on-worship, accessed October 1, 2013.

64. N. T. Wright, http://resurrectedliving.wordpress.com /2013/06/11/some-collected-quotes-on-worship-2, accessed October 1, 2013.

65. C. S. Lewis, *Reflections on the Psalms* (New York: Mariner Books, 1964). http://christiananswers.net/ dictionary/ worship.html, accessed October 1, 2013.

66. Foster, *Celebration of Discipline*, 164.

67. Thompson, *Anatomy of the Soul*.

68. Calhoun, 27.

Further Resources

Books

Anderson, Kelli Ra. *Divine Duct Tape: Transforming Every Day Life into Real Life with Christ.* St. Charles: Foxburrow Media, 2011.

Barry, William A., and William J. Connolly. *The Practice of Spiritual Direction.* New York: Harper One, 2009.

Becker, Amy Julia. *A Good and Perfect Gift: Faith, Expectations, and a Little Girl Named Penny.* Grand Rapids: Bethany House, 2011.

Bolduc, Kathleen Deyer. *His Name is Joel: Searching for God in a Son's Disability.* Louisville, KY: Bridge Resources, 1999.

——. *A Place Called Acceptance: Ministry with Families of Children with Disabilities.* Louisville, KY: Bridge Resources, 2001.

——. *Autism & Alleluias.* Valley Forge: Judson Press, 2010.

Colson, Emily, and Charles W. Colson. *Dancing with Max: A Mother and Son Who Broke Free.* Grand Rapids: Zondervan, 2010.

Ferrini, Joe, and Cindi Ferrini. *Unexpected Journey: When Special Needs Change Our Course.* Cleveland: Morris, 2009.

Fryling, Alice. *Seeking God Together: An Introduction to Group Spiritual Direction.* Downers Grove, IL: InterVarsity, 2009.

Hausmann, Margot. *Multisensory Worship Ideas*, rwjms.umdnj.edu/boggscenter/projects/documents/MultisensoryWorshipIdeas.pdf.

Hubach, Stephanie O. *Same Lake, Different Boat: Coming alongside People Touched by Disability.* Phillipsburg, NJ: P&R, 2006.

Langston, Kelly. *Autism's Hidden Blessings: Discovering God's Promises for Autistic Children and Their Families.* Grand Rapids: Kregel, 2009.

Marchenko, Gillian. Sun Shine Down: A Memoir. Ossining, NY: T.S. Poetry Press, 2013.

Myers, Patty Corrigan. *Autism Is a Blessing: A Family's Struggle with Autism and How They Found the Blessings*. Mustang, OK: Tate, 2008.

Nouwen, Henri J. M. *Adam: God's Beloved*. Maryknoll, NY: Orbis, 1997.

———. *Spiritual Direction: Wisdom for the Long Walk of Faith*. New York: HarperCollins, 2006.

Philo, Jolene. *Different Dream Parenting: A Practical Guide to Raising a Child with Special Needs*. Grand Rapids: Discovery House, 2011.

Rupp, Joyce. *The Cup of Our Lives: A Guide for Spiritual Growth*. Notre Dame, IN: Ave Maria, 1997.

Wiederkehr, Macrina, OSB. *Abide: Keeping Vigil with the Word of God*. Collegeville, MN: Liturgical, 2011.

Websites and Blogs

American Association of Persons with Disabilities Interfaith Initiative: www.aapd.com/what-we-do/interfaith/interfaith-initiative.html

Chosen Families: www.chosenfamilies.org

Kathleen Deyer Bolduc: www.kathleenbolduc.com

Barbara Crooker: www.barbaracrooker.com

Barbara Dittrich: www.comfortinthemidstofchaos.com

Joe and Cindi Ferrini: cindiferrini.com

Not-Alone: www.specialneedsparenting.net

Occasional Sightings of the Gospel: occasionalsightings.blogspot.com

Religion and Spirituality Division of the American Association of Intellectual and Developmental Disabilities: www.aaiddreligion.org

Snappin' Ministries: A Special Needs Parent Network: www.snappin.org

For this reason I bow my knees before the Father, from whom every family in heaven and on earth takes its name. I pray that, according to the riches of his glory, he may grant that you may be strengthened in your inner being with power through his Spirit, and that Christ may dwell in your hearts through faith, as you are being rooted and grounded in love. I pray that you may have the power to comprehend, with all the saints, what is the breadth and length and height and depth, and to know the love of Christ that surpasses knowledge, so that you may be filled with all the fullness of God. Now to him who by the power at work within us is able to accomplish abundantly far more than all we can ask or imagine, to him be glory in the church and in Christ Jesus to all generations, forever and ever. Amen.

—Ephesians 3:14-21 NRSV